A
NEW TESTAMENT
WORDBOOK

A NEW TESTAMENT WORDBOOK

WILLIAM BARCLAY

What benefit can we reap from this munificence, if we have not the meaning of the words explained to us?

GREGORY OF NYSSA,
Sermons on the Beatitudes, I

SCM PRESS LTD
56 BLOOMSBURY STREET
LONDON

To

J.P. and G.A.D.

who taught me
to know Greek a little
and to love Greek much

First published November 1955
Reprinted March 1956
Reprinted August 1956
Reprinted January 1959

Printed in Great Britain by
Northumberland Press Limited
Gateshead on Tyne

FOREWORD

WILLIAM BARCLAY is a teacher. In Trinity College in the University of Glasgow, he teaches New Testament to men in preparation for the ministry of the Church of Scotland.

If my memory serves me well, not all teachers are good at their jobs. William Barclay does what I think a good teacher ought to do, he illuminates. The pieces in this book appeared on the page he writes each week in the *British Weekly*. I supposed when it began that it would be read by ministers who tried to toss an occasional Greek word into a sermon to convince their congregations that some years in a theological college had been not entirely lost on them. But the letters came from quite a different quarter. A horticulturist who is an expert on compost wrote the first letter. He wanted William Barclay's Word Book—as we call it—in 'more permanent form'. Old ladies who sit in their windows and watch the sea, school masters in the interior of British Columbia, Sunday School teachers in Wigan and the West Country, solicitors in the Midlands and the South of England, ministers in places with names like Wenatchee and Nanaimo, readers in Holland and Sweden, and teachers in other theological colleges, wrote by the dozen every week and asked for this book to be made.

There is a not unimportant lesson in this. There was no reason to suppose that thousands of ordinary people who had never heard a Greek word that they knew to be Greek, were waiting for a scholar to instruct them. This particular scholar, however, was so saturated in the things he knew, so excited by them also, and he was at the same time so in touch with the people to whom he wanted to tell what he knew, that he brought them together with ease.

Perhaps those who talk about 'the problem of communication' can learn something from William Barclay—that to communicate anything, it is necessary to know it and to know equally the people to whom we wish to communicate it. That may be why William Barclay is not only a great teacher but a great preacher.

There is no doubt that the author of this book is right when he speaks in his Preface of the 'quite extraordinary interest in the Bible which exists to-day'. The very existence of the opportunity puts us even more deeply in the debt of a man like this who teaches us also how to use it.

SHAUN HERRON

London

CONTENTS

ABBREVIATIONS

NT New Testament
OT Old Testament
AV Authorized Version
RSV Revised Standard Version

PREFACE

It would be true to say that this book began almost accidentally. Words are always fascinating things. I was asked a few years ago by a parish minister if I would write three short articles on three great NT words for his congregational magazine, and I did so. At that time another series of articles which I was writing for the *British Weekly* was coming to an end, and I had to think of something with which to follow it. I suggested to Mr. Shaun Herron, the editor of that weekly, that I might experiment with a series of word articles in his columns. He agreed, and that series of articles has been running ever since. I wish to say that I am deeply grateful to him, first, for allowing me space in the *British Weekly* for these word articles, and second, for giving me permission to republish them in this form. Had it not been for his continual encouragement that series would never have begun and this book would never have been written.

As the series went on it became clear that there were many people who wished to possess the articles in more permanent form. At first I was surprised at this, for these articles might be defined as an attempt to popularize the Greek dictionary, and to teach Greek to people who do not know any Greek. But it seems to me that this interest was simply one facet of the quite extraordinary interest in the Bible which exists to-day and which is becoming ever stronger. I do not think that there ever was a time when people were more interested in what the Bible has to say and in what the Bible means.

Therein lies the justification for a book like this. Translation from one language into another is in one sense impossible. It is always possible to translate words with accuracy when they refer to *things*. A chair is a chair in any language. But it is a different matter when it is a question of *ideas*. In that case some words need, not another to translate them, but a phrase, or a sentence, or even a paragraph. Further, words have associations. They have associations with people, with history, with ideas, with other words, and these associations give words a certain flavour which cannot be rendered in translation, but which affects their meaning and significance in the most important way. This book is an attempt to take certain great NT words and to find out what these words meant to the writers of the NT and to those who read and heard their message for the first time. To do that means seeking to trace the meaning of these words in classical Greek, in the Septuagint, when they occur there, in hellenistic Greek and in the papyri.

Since these terms are constantly used in these word studies, it will be well to explain them at the beginning. It may be said the classical Greek comes to an end in 300 B.C. From then until A.D. 300 may be taken as the age of hellenistic Greek. During that age Greek became the language of the world. The conquests of Alexander the Great took the Greek language everywhere. A situation arose in which people, in their private and domestic life, spoke their own native tongue, but in business and commercial and public life they spoke Greek. The extent to which this was true can be seen that in those days many people had two names. It might be that one was the name in their own tongue, and the other was a translation of that name into Greek. So *Cephas* is the Hebrew for a 'rock', and *Peter* is the Greek for the same word. *Thomas* is the Hebrew for a 'twin', and *Didymus* is the Greek for the same word. It might be that the Greek name was taken because it was like the native name in sound. So a Jew called *Eliakim* or *Abel* became in Greek society Alcimus or Apelles. Now this Greek which spread all over the world was not classical Greek. It was a kind of simplified Greek with the irregularities and the dialectic peculiarities and the subtle nuances of Greek moods and tenses ironed out. It was called the *Koinē*, which is short for *hē koinē dialektos*, the common tongue. It would be wrong to think of it as a debased form of Greek; it is still a beautiful, flexible language, but it is a form of Greek simplified to meet the needs of a world and not of a country or nation.

The Septuagint is the Greek version of the OT. The translation was begun in Alexandria about 275 B.C. By that time the Jews of the Dispersion were far more familiar with Greek than they were with the original Hebrew. The Septuagint is of the greatest importance because it was the Bible of the Christian Church before the NT came to be written. Very often when the NT writers quote the OT it is the Septuagint which they use, and not the original Hebrew. The language of the Septuagint therefore became entwined in Christian thought.

Of all sources the papyri throw the most vivid light on the language of the NT. Papyrus was a writing material made from the pith of a bulrush which grew on the banks of the Nile. It was made by cutting the pith into strips and pressing the strips together. So long as it does not become damp it lasts practically for ever. It was the universal writing material of NT times. In Egypt writings on papyrus were thrown on the rubbish heaps; the desert sands drifted over them and buried them; and they can still be dug up and deciphered to-day. The papyri contain things like census and tax returns, marriage and trade contracts, schoolboys' exercises, petitions to the government, and, above all, private letters. In the papyri we see the Greek language as the ordinary, non-literary person of NT times spoke it. We see how words were used, and what significance they had, not in careful literary prose, but in everyday speech.

He who writes about words is obviously dependent on the labours of others, and the following is a list of the books which I have constantly used.

LEXICONS AND CONCORDANCES:

H. G. Liddell and R. Scott, *A Greek-English Lexicon,* revised and augmented by Sir H. S. Jones.

Gerhard Kittel, *Theologisches Wörterbuch zum Neuen Testament.*

Erwin Preuschen, *Handwörterbuch zum Griechischen Neuen Testament.*

J. H. Moulton and G. Milligan, *The Vocabulary of the Greek*

Testament, illustrated from the papyri and other non-literary sources.

W. F. Moulton and A. S. Geden, *A Concordance to the Greek Testament.*

J. H. Thayer, *A Greek-English Lexicon of the New Testament,* being Grimm's Wilke's *Clavis Novi Testamenti,* translated and enlarged by J. H. Thayer.

G. Abbott-Smith, *Manual Greek Lexicon of the New Testament.*

Hesychius, *Hesychii Alexandrini Lexicon,* ed. M. Schmidt.

Suidas, *Suidae Lexicon,* ed. I. Bekker.

E. A. Sophocles, *Greek Lexicon of the Roman and Byzantine Periods.*

E. J. Goodspeed, *Index Patristicus.*

E. Hatch and H. A. Redpath, *A Concordance to the Septuagint.*

GENERAL WORKS:

M. David and B. A. van Groningen, *Papyrological Primer.*

A. Deissmann, *Light from the Ancient East,* E.T. by L. R. M. Strachan.
Bible Studies, E.T. by A. Grieve.

F. Field, *Notes on the Translation of the New Testament.*

E. Hatch, *Essays in Biblical Greek.*

H. A. A. Kennedy, *Sources of New Testament Greek.*

A. S. Hunt and G. C. Edgar, *Select Papyri,* two volumes, *Loeb Classical Library.*

H. G. Meecham, *Light from Ancient Letters.*

G. Milligan, *Here and There among the Papyri.*
Selections from the Greek Papyri.

J. H. Moulton, *From Egyptian Rubbish Heaps.*

E. K. Simpson, *Words worth weighing in the Greek New Testament.*

R. C. Trench, *Synonyms of the New Testament.*

J. G. Winter, *Life and Letters in the Papyri.*

S. Witkowski, *Epistulae privatae Graecae quae in papyris aetatis Lagidarum servantur.*

I should like to think of this book as an attempt to make

the results of linguistic scholarship available for the ordinary reader of the NT. It is my hope and my prayer that it may do something to make the NT more meaningful for at least some than it was before.

WILLIAM BARCLAY

Trinity College
Glasgow

NOTE ON THE TRANSLITERATION AND PRONUNCIATION OF GREEK WORDS

For the most part Greek letters are commonly pronounced as in English. But there are certain things which ought to be noted.

(i) Greek has four letters which represent more than a single letter in English. These four letters are *phi, psi, chi* and *theta*; they are transliterated respectively, *ph, ps, ch* and *th*.

(ii) Two of the Greek vowels have a double sound. *Omicron* and *omega* both represent the English letter *o*. But *omicron* represents a short *o* as in the word *hot*, and *omega* represents a long *o* as in the word *go*. In this book *o* represents *omicron*, and *ō* represents *omega*. Similarly *epsilon* represents a short *e* as in the word *get*, and *eta* represents a long *e*, which is pronounced as the *a* in *hate*, or as the *ee* in *feet*. In this book *e* represents *epsilon* and *ē* represents *eta*.

(iii) When two *g*'s come together in Greek they are pronounced *ng*. So *aggelos* (*messenger* or *angel*) is pronounced *angelos*.

AGGAREUEIN

THE WORD OF AN OCCUPIED COUNTRY

THERE are some words which carry in their history the story of a nation's triumph or a nation's tragedy. *Aggareuein* is such a word. It is used three times in the NT, with the meaning to *compel*. It is the word used in Matt. 5.41 when Jesus speaks of going two miles when we are *compelled* to go one; and in Matt. 27.32 and Mark 15.21 it is the word that is used of Simon of Cyrene being *compelled* to carry the Cross of Jesus to Calvary.

In origin the word is Persian; it comes from the noun *aggaros*, which means a 'courier'; it became naturalized into Greek, just as the Italian word *estafette* has been to some extent naturalized into English with the same sense of a 'military courier' or an 'express messenger'. The Persians had a remarkably efficient courier system, like an express post. Herodotus has a description of it (Herodotus 8.98). 'Nothing travels so fast as these Persian messengers. The entire plan is a Persian invention; and this is the method of it. Along the whole line of road there are men (they say) stationed with horses, in number equal to the number of days which the journey takes, allowing a man and a horse to each day; and these men will not be hindered from accomplishing at their best speed the distance which they have to go, either by snow, or rain, or heat, or by the darkness of the night. The first rider delivers his despatch to the second, and the second passes it to the third; and so it is borne from hand to hand along the whole line, like the light in the torch race. . . . The Persians give the riding post in this manner the name *aggareion*.' Xenophon has an even more vivid description of it (*Cyropaedia* 8.6.17). He says that Cyrus had to find some way of finding out what was going on in his vast empire. He experimented and found out how far a horse and rider could go in one day without breaking down, and so arranged his stations. At each station there was a permanent official to see to the transference of the letters and to change the horses. Night and day this express service went on. 'It is undeniable,' says Xenophon, 'that this is the fastest overland travelling on earth.' Aeschylus in the *Agamemnon* tells how there came to Greece news of the capture of Troy. The chorus will hardly believe Clytaemnestra that word could have come so quickly. She tells how the news was transmitted by torch from Ida to Lemnos, from Athos to Olympus by what she calls 'the courier fire' (*aggarou puros*). Now it was the law that anyone could be compelled to provide a horse or to act as guide to keep this service going. And therefore *aggareuein* came to mean 'forcibly to impress some one to service', to compel him to serve whether he liked it or not. In an occupied country that was a grave and serious thing. Anyone could be impressed to carry the baggage of the army for a certain distance; anyone could be compelled to perform any service that the occupiers chose to lay upon him. That is what happened to Simon of Cyrene. This business of impressment was one of the bitterest and most constant humiliations that subject nations had to endure. Epictetus (4.1.79) is talking about how a man must submit to whatever the gods lay upon him. He may not even desire health, if the gods wish to take it away. 'You ought to possess your whole body as a paltry ass with a pack-saddle on, as long as may be, as long as it is allowed you. But if there should come an act of impressment (*aggareia*) and a soldier should lay hold on it, let it go. Do not resist or murmur. If you do, you will first be beaten and lose the ass after all.' A man had no appeal when this humiliation came upon him.

How humiliating this could be, and how this *aggareia* was abused can be seen in the regulations that governments had to make to curb the exercise of it. When Demetrius of Syria was wooing the Jews in the times of the Maccabaean Jonathan, Josephus says (*Antiquities*, 13.2.3) that he offered to abolish many taxes, such as the salt tax and the poll tax, and 'I also give order that the beasts of the Jews be not "impressed" (*aggareuein*) into our service'. From the papyri we learn that in Egypt boats for instance, and cattle and labour were regularly 'impressed'. Ptolemy Euergetēs the second and his queen decree that his governors and officials 'shall not impress any of the inhabitants of the country for private services, nor requisition (*aggareuein*) their cattle for any purpose of their own', and that, 'No one shall requisition boats (*aggareuein*) for his own use on any pretext whatsoever'. In the Temple of the Great Oasis in Egypt there was an inscription, in which Capito, the prefect of Egypt, admitted that soldiers had made illegal requisitions and laid it down that 'no one shall take or requisition (*aggareuein*) anything, unless he has a written authorization from me'. It is quite clear that the local and the military officials requisitioned both things and people, not only for the public services and for the army's purposes, but for their own private convenience and profit.

Now it is even clearer what Jesus is saying in the Sermon on the Mount (Matt. 5.41). He is saying: 'If someone exacts from you the most distasteful and humiliating service, if someone compels you to do something that invades your rights and that he has no right to ask, if you are treated like a defenceless victim in an occupied country, don't resent it. Do what you are asked and do even more, and do it with good will, for such is my way.' A generation which is for ever standing on its rights might well think of that.

APECHEIN

PAYMENT IN FULL

IN the NT there are certainly three, and perhaps five, extremely interesting technical usages of the word *apechein*. The main part of the word is the verb *echein*, which means 'to have'.

In Matt 6.2, 6, 16, Jesus says of those who give alms ostentatiously, of those who pray in such a way that everyone will see them, and of those who make a parade of their fasting: 'Verily I say unto you, *they have their reward.*' (*Apechousin* [the present indicative of *apechein*] *ton misthon.*) This word *apechein* is the technical Greek word for 'receiving payment in full'. Sometimes it is used in a general sense. Callimachus (Epigram, 51) speaks of a certain Miccus, who paid all honour to his aged nurse Aeschra. He 'cared for her in her old age with all good things, and when she died he set up her statue for future generations to see, so that the old woman has received thanks (*apechei charitas*) for her nursing breasts'. She received in full the grateful reward for her tender care. Callimachus (Epigram, 55) has another epigram in which he speaks of a certain Aceson, who has set up a tablet to Asclepius, the god of healing, in gratitude for his wife's recovery from illness. 'Know, Asclepius, that thou hast received the debt (*chreos apecheis*) which Aceson owed thee by his vow for his wife Demodice. But if thou dost forget and demand payment again, this tablet says it will bear witness.' The tablet is the witness that the debt is paid in full. In his life of Solon (ch. 22) Plutarch tells how Solon, to check immorality, made a law that an illegitimate son need not support his father. Then he goes on to say of the father, 'he has his reward (*misthon echei*) in that he robs himself of all right to upbraid his sons for neglecting him, since he has made their very existence a reproach to them'. The sinning father has received full pay for his sin. In his life of Themistocles (ch. 17) Plutarch tells how Themistocles won the admiration of all. Sparta gave him the prize for wisdom. At the Olympic games the crowds gazed on him rather than on the competitors, and pointed him out to visiting strangers, 'so that Themistocles was delighted and confessed to his friends that he was now reaping in full measure the harvest (*ton karpon apechein*) of his toils for Hellas'. The admiration of the people was payment in full for all his toils.

But *apechein* has a still more technical use. It was the technical word which was used for 'receipting an account' which had been paid in full. It is the equivalent of the English phrase 'received payment of . . .' Deissmann and Moulton and Milligan provide ample examples of this use of the word in every connection. It is used in connection with 'the payment of rent'. Asclepiades, a landowner, writes to Portis, his tenant: 'Asclepiades, the son of Charmagon, to Portis, the son of Permamis, greeting. I have *received* from you the fruit that falls to me (rents were paid in kind) (*apechō*) and the increase of the lot that I have let to you, for the sowing of the year 25, and I have no further claims to make on you.' 'I have *received* from you the rent of the olive-press which you have from me on hire.' It is used in connection with 'the payment of taxes'. A resident alien had to pay a tax and a receipt for such a tax runs as follows: 'Pamaris, the son of Hermodorus, to Abos. I have *received* from you the alien tax for the months of Thouth and Phaophi. In the year 19 of Tiberius Caesar Augustus.' It is used in connection with 'the payment of religious dues'. 'Psenamunis, the son of Pekusis, to the labourer under contract, Pibuchis, the son of Pateesis, greeting. I have *received* from you 4 drachmae and 1 obol (about 3s. 8d.) being the collection of Isis, on behalf of the public works.' It is used in connection with 'the payment of the price for a slave'. So the seller writes: 'I have *received* the whole price.' In all business transactions *apechein* is the normal word for 'receiving payment in full'.

So what Jesus is saying is that those who give alms and pray and fast in such a way that they deliberately seek the admiration of men, receive the admiration of men—*and that is all*. The admiration of men is their payment in full. They have no further claim; they can write their receipt and consider themselves paid in full. The thing may win the admiration of man, but when it is designed to do so, it is of no value to God. If we aim at personal publicity, we get it—but we get nothing more. By getting it we are paid in full, but we miss completely the far greater rewards of God which are given to humble and selfless and self-effacing service.

The two not so certain instances are, first, Philem. 15. Paul there writes to Philemon that perhaps he lost the runaway Onesimus for a short time, that he might receive him (*apechein*) for ever. If Philemon will only take Onesimus back as a Christian brother, he may have lost him in this temporary world as a slave, but he will receive full payment, by receiving him for ever as a brother. The second instance is of great interest. In Mark 14.41 when Jesus has emerged victorious from His agony in the Garden, He says, as the AV has it, '*It is enough*; the hour is come; the Son of Man is betrayed into the hands of sinners.' And then verse 43 goes on to describe the arrival of Judas. Now the phrase which is translated, 'It is enough', is the one Greek word *apechei*. And it may well mean, not 'It is enough', but it may be a reference to Judas. Jesus may have pointed to him and said: '*He has been paid his money in full*. The traitor is here.' Jesus may well have been saying to Judas: 'Is this the payment in full which you have been looking for?' And so Jesus may have been trying to remind Judas that there was an account with Himself and with God still to be settled.

APOBLEPEIN, APHORAN AND ATENIZEIN

THE STEADFAST GAZE

Apoblepein is used in the NT only twice, and *aphoran* only once, but they are such vivid words that they repay the closest study. They are to all intents and purposes synonyms and both of them mean the same thing and have much the same history. Both *blepein* and *horan* mean 'to see' or 'to look'; and *apo*, which is the first part of both of these words, means 'away from'; and both words mean 'to look away from everything else in order to focus one's gaze on one thing'; they mean to neglect everything else in order to concentrate one's attention on one thing.

The important instance of *apoblepein* is in Heb. 11.26. There it is said that Moses gave up the pleasure and the ease and the luxury that he might have enjoyed with the Egyptians in order to identify himself with the struggles and the sorrows of his own people; and he is said to have done this because 'he had respect unto the recompense of the reward'. The American RSV puts it, 'For he looked to the reward'; Moffatt puts it, 'for he had an eye to the reward'. The meaning is that he turned away from the rewards of earth to concentrate on the reward of heaven.

The one instance of *aphoran* is in Heb. 12.2, where we are enjoined to run 'looking unto Jesus'. Moffatt translates it, 'our eyes fixed upon Jesus'; the American RSV translates it, 'looking to Jesus'. Moffatt, in his commentary on Hebrews, suggests the translation, 'with no eyes for anyone but Jesus'. The idea is that we are to withdraw our gaze from everyone else to gaze at Jesus.

But to get the full flavour of these words, let us look at their usage in Greek.

First, let us look at *apoblepein*. Suidas, the Greek lexicon, tells us that *apoblepein* is used by Aeschines as a synonym of *thaumazein*, which means 'to wonder'. Philostratus tells us that when Apollonius, the famous sophist, landed in Egypt, as he advanced from the ship the people 'gazed at him' (*apoblepein*) as a god. When Xenophon is telling of a man whose services the country was needing, he says, Your fatherland is 'looking' (*apoblepein*) to you. Philo describes the builder, as building and all the while 'looking' (*apoblepein*) into the pattern of the architect. Xenophon speaks of a person as being so vain that she kept 'gazing' (*apoblepein*) at her own reflection. Plato says that it is the aim of the lover to make the loved one so dependent on him that the lover in all things 'will look' (*apoblepein*) to him in utter love and complete dependence. An Ephesian inscription tells of one who 'looked' (*apoblepein*) to the reverence of the gods and to the honour of the most illustrious city of the Ephesians. Theophrastus in his *Characters* uses *apoblepein* to describe the look of the flatterer who gazes with rapt attention at the person he wishes to impress.

Now let us look at *aphoran*. Lucian uses it for one man looking intently at another as they pursued an argument. Twice Epictetus uses it. He uses it in a description of his aims with his pupils. 'And so now I am your teacher, and you are being taught in my school. And my purpose is this —to make of you a perfect work, secure against restraint, compulsion and hindrance, free, prosperous, happy, looking to (*aphoran*) God in everything both great and small.' He describes the great hero and benefactor Hercules as 'looking to' (*aphoran*) Zeus in everything he did. Josephus, describing the death of Aaron, tells how, as he died, the crowd 'looked wonderingly' (*aphoran*) upon him.

From all this there emerges a wonderful picture of the way in which the true Christian looks at the blessedness of God and the wonder of Jesus Christ. He looks with an utter fixity of concentration; he looks with wondering amazement; he looks as one who looks to a champion and a saviour; he looks as one who looks at the master plan and pattern of life; he looks as a loved one looks with adoration at his lover; he looks as a man looks at his familiar friend; he looks as a man looks to God when God has become for him the only reality in the world.

Aphoran and *apoblepein* describe the look of the soul which is 'lost in wonder, love and praise'.

There is another NT word which implies a fixity of gaze. It is the word *atenizein*, which means 'to gaze intently at'. It is a favourite word of Luke. It occurs fourteen times in the NT; of these fourteen instances two are in II Cor. (3.7, 13), two are in the Gospel according to St. Luke, and the remaining ten are in Acts.

It is used of the people in the Synagogue of Nazareth gazing with intent bewilderment at Jesus (Luke 4.20). It is used of the close scrutiny of the servant in the courtyard of the High Priest's house when Peter was recognized (Luke 22.56). It is used of the disciples gazing after Jesus when the ascension had taken place (Acts 1.10). It is used of Peter's and John's gaze at the lame man at the Temple gate (Acts 3.4), and of the astonished gaze of the people at them after the miracle had taken place (Acts 3.12). It is used of the Sanhedrin gazing at Stephen as he spoke with eloquence and debated with power (Acts 6.15), and of Stephen's own gaze up into heaven as he died beneath the stones of the mob (Acts 7.55). It is used of Peter's astonished gaze at the angel who warned him of the coming of Cornelius (Acts 10.4), and of his gaze at the vision of the creatures on the sheet (Acts 11.6). It is used of Paul's penetrating look at

Elymas, the hostile sorcerer (Acts 13.9). It is used of the look of dawning hope in the eyes of the lame man at Lystra (Acts 14.9). It is used of Paul's piercing look at the Sanhedrin (Acts 23.1). And it is used of the way in which the people looked at Moses when he came down from the mount, or rather of the way in which it was impossible for them to look at him because of the divine glory that shone from him (II Cor. 3.7, 13).

It can, therefore, be seen that this word *atenizein* expresses a look of astonishment and amazement, a look of scrutiny ending in recognition, a look of wonder, a look of expectation and hope, and a look of sheer, piercing authority. Now the interesting thing is that when we come to the writings of Clement of Rome, who wrote towards the very end of the first Christian century, and who was the first of the apostolic fathers and one of the great leaders of the Church, we find that he does not use *apoblepein* or *aphoran,* but that he is notably fond of this word *atenizein.* We find that he uses it in three notable connections.

(i) First of all in his first letter to the Corinthians, chapter 36, he urges the Christian to gaze steadfastly (*atenizein*) at the heights of the heavens. In a tempting and a hostile world the Christian's gaze must be fixed on heaven.

(ii) Second, he uses it of God. In the same letter in chapter 19, he says, 'Let is fix our gaze (*atenizein*) on the Father and Creator of the whole universe.' God must be the object of the Christian's thought and contemplation.

(iii) Third, he uses it of Jesus Christ. In the same letter in chapter 7, he says, 'Let us fix our gaze (*atenizein*) upon the blood of Christ, and let us know how costly it is to his Father, because it was poured out for our salvation.' The Christian must fix his eyes upon the wounded and the crucified Christ.

The word is different from *apoblepein* and *aphoran,* but the thought is precisely the same. In a world where it was hard to be a Christian, a world where the tainting pollutions sought to infect the Christians on every side, a world where Christians had already died terribly for their faith, the one thing necessary was the steadfast gaze upon heaven and God and Jesus Christ. That alone could enable a Christian man to remain a Christian—and it is still so.

ARRABŌN

THE FORETASTE OF WHAT IS TO COME

THE word *arrabōn* has one of the most human and interesting backgrounds of all NT words. It is used only by Paul, and it was a favourite word of his because he uses it three times, always in the same connection. In II Cor. 1.22 he says that God has given us the *arrabōn* of the Holy Spirit in our hearts. In II Cor. 5.5 he again talks about the *arrabōn* of the Holy Spirit. And in Eph. 1.14 he speaks about the Holy Spirit being the *arrabōn* of our inheritance. In each of these cases the AV translates the word *arrabōn* by the English word 'earnest'. Moffatt translates it 'pledge' and 'instalment'. The American RSV translates it 'guarantee'.

In classical Greek the word *arrabōn* regularly means the caution money that a purchaser had to deposit and pay down when a bargain was struck and which was forfeited if the purchase was not carried out. It was the first instalment which was the pledge and guarantee that the rest would follow in due time.

The word is very common in the papyri in business documents and agreements. Milligan quotes some very interesting usages of it. We take three of them as examples. A woman was selling a cow and she received one thousand drachmae as an *arrabōn* that the remainder of the price would be paid. Certain dancing girls were being hired for a village festival and they are paid so many drachmae in advance as an *arrabōn*, with proviso that this already paid sum will be taken into account when the final payment is made after the performance has been given. And—a rather amusing instance—a man writes, 'Regarding Lampōn, the mouse-catcher, I paid him for you as *arrabōn* eight drachmae in order that he may catch the mice while they are with young.' The advance payment is made, as a guarantee of full payment, so that Lampōn will get on with the job of catching mice while the going is good! So then in secular Greek contemporary with the NT *arrabōn* is regularly a part payment which is an assurance and a guarantee that full payment will follow; it is an instalment paid down in advance which is the proof and the pledge that the whole sum will in due course be forthcoming.

Now Paul's use of the word is always as a description of the Holy Spirit. So what Paul is saying is that God's gift to us of the Holy Spirit here and now is an instalment, a guarantee, an advance foretaste of the life which the Christian will some day live when he lives in the presence of God.

Paul spoke out of a Jewish background. To a Jew the Holy Spirit of God had two great functions. (i) It was through His Holy Spirit that God spoke to man. The prophet spoke because the Spirit of the Lord was on him. It was God's Holy Spirit who revealed to Simeon that he would see God's Anointed One before he died (Luke 2.25). (ii) But also, it was God's Holy Spirit in his heart which enabled a man to recognize God's truth when he heard it. The Jews believed that the Holy Spirit of God operated from *without* to bring men truth; and from *within* to enable them to recognize truth. The Holy Spirit was at once, to them, the revealer and the touchstone of truth.

So when Paul uses the word *arrabōn* of the Holy Spirit the thought in his mind is that the imperfect knowledge that men now possess is the first instalment of the full knowledge they will one day possess; that which God has told them now is the pledge and guarantee that He will some day tell them all; that the joy that comes to a man now in the Spirit is the pledge of the perfect joy of heaven. The Holy Spirit to Paul is the guarantee of God that, though now we see through a glass darkly, we shall some day see face to face; and that, though now we only know in part, we shall some day know even as we are known (I Cor. 13.12).

ASELGEIA

THE UTTER SHAMELESSNESS

IN many ways *aselgeia* is the ugliest word in the list of NT sins. It occurs quite frequently (Mark 7.22; II Cor. 12.21; Gal. 5.19; Eph. 4.19; I Pet. 4.3; Jude 4; Rom. 13.13; II Pet. 2.2, 7, 18). The AV varies between 'lasciviousness' and 'wantonness'. The RSV consistently prefers 'licentiousness'. Moffatt regularly translates it 'sensuality'. To some extent all these translations fail to give the one essential characteristic of *aselgeia*.

Let us look first at some of the classical and Christian definitions of it. It is used by Plato in the sense of 'impudence'. It is defined by a late writer as 'preparedness for every pleasure'. It is defined as 'violence coupled with insult and audacity'. It is defined by Basil as 'a disposition of the soul which does not possess and cannot bear the pain of discipline'. It is described as 'the spirit which knows no restraints and which dares whatever caprice and wanton insolence suggest'. It is Lightfoot who seizes on the essential quality in *aselgeia*. He says that a man may be 'unclean' (*akathartos*) and hide his sin, but the man who is *aselgēs* (the adjective) shocks public decency. Here is the very essence of *aselgeia*; the man in whose soul *aselgeia* dwells is so much in the grip of sin, so much under its domination, that he does not care what people say or think so long as he can gratify his evil desire. He is the man who is lost to shame. Most men have enough decency left to seek to hide their sin, but the *aselgēs* is long past that. He will be guilty of any outrageous conduct, and care for nothing except to satisfy his desires. He is like a drug-taker. At first the drug-taker will indulge secretly and will try to conceal the fact that he takes drugs at all. In the end he will whine and grovel and beg and beseech and implore completely without restraint and completely without shame, because the drug has so mastered him.

Now it so happens that, in the NT, *aselgeia* usually

occurs, not alone, but either in lists of sins or in conjunction with other sins. It is instructive to see with what other sins it is most closely connected.

(i) Three times (Mark 7.22; Eph. 4.19; II Pet. 2.2) it occurs close to *pleonexia*. *Pleonexia* is the unbridled longing to possess more, the uncontrollable desire to possess things which are forbidden and which should not be desired at all. Therefore there is in *aselgeia* the idea of 'sheer, shameless greed'. It is the vice of the man who will submit to demean himself and to shame himself in any way in order to possess that which he has set his heart upon.

(ii) In four cases (Mark 7.22; II Cor. 12.21; Gal. 5.19; II Pet. 2.18) it is connected with adultery and lust and sexual sin. Therefore in *aselgeia* there is involved the idea of 'sheer animal lust'. One has only to walk the streets of any great city to see that kind of *aselgeia* in terrible action. It is the vice of a man who has no more shame than an animal in the gratification of his physical desires.

(iii) In three cases (Gal. 5.19; I Pet. 4.3; Rom. 13.13) it is connected with drunkenness. In particular it is connected with the word *kōmoi*. Originally a *kōmos* was a band of friends who accompanied a victor in the games on his way home. They sang their rejoicings and his praises. But the word degenerated until it came to mean a 'carousal', a band of drunken revellers, swaying and singing their way through the streets. Therefore *aselgeia* has in it that 'sheer self-indulgence', which is such a slave to its so-called pleasures that it is lost to shame.

It is perhaps Josephus who gives us the flavour of the meaning of *aselgeia* best of all. He couples it with *mania*, 'madness', and he declares that that was the sin of Jezebel when she erected a shrine of Baal in the Holy City, the very city of God. Such an act was a shocking outrage which defied all decency and flaunted all public opinion. *Aselgeia* is a grim word. It is the wanton insolence that is lost to shame. It is a grim commentary on human nature that a man can be so mastered by sin that in the end he loses even shame.

CHARISMA

THE GIFT OF GOD

Charisma basically means 'a gift'. Outside the NT it is not at all a common word. In classical Greek it is rare. It is not common in the papyri, but there is one suggestive occurrence where a man classifies his property as that which he acquired *apo agorasias*, 'by purchase', and that which he acquired *apo charismatos*, 'by gift'. In the NT *charisma* is a characteristically Pauline word. Altogether it occurs seventeen times, fourteen times in the undoubted Pauline letters, twice in the Pastoral Epistles, and once in I Peter.

(i) It is used of what we might call 'gifts of grace'. Paul longs to visit Rome in order to impart to the Romans some *charisma* (Rom. 1.11). The Corinthians are deficient in no *charisma* (I Cor. 1.7). He bids them covet the best *charismata* (I Cor. 12.31) and then goes on to sing his hymn to love. *Charismata* are the graces of the Christian life.

(ii) It is used of God's 'grace and forgiveness' in that situation where judgment and condemnation would have been only just. In Rom. 5.15, 16, man's sin and God's *charisma* of gracious forgiveness are contrasted. In Rom. 6.23—a verse to which we shall return—the wages of sin is death, but the *charisma* of God is eternal life.

(iii) It is used of the 'natural endowments' which a man possesses. Every man, says Paul, has his own *charisma* from God (I Cor. 7.7). Peter exhorts every man to serve others as he has received his *charisma* (I Pet. 4.10).

(iv) It is used of 'the gift which is implanted in a man when he is ordained to the ministry'. Timothy must never neglect the gift that came to him by the laying on of hands by the Presbytery (I Tim. 4.14, cp. II Tim. 1.6). The gift of God comes to men through the hands of men, but it remains a gift of God.

(v) It is specially used for all 'the special gifts which can be exercised in the service of the Church'. There are two great lists of these gifts. Rom. 12.6-8 lists prophecy, ministry, teaching, exhortation, giving, ruling, showing mercy. I Cor. 12.8-10 is a longer list. I Cor. 12.28-30 points out how different *charismata* are given to different people.

(vi) It is used for 'God's rescue in a difficult situation' (II Cor. 1.11).

The whole basic idea of the word is that of a free and undeserved gift, of something given to a man unearned and unmerited, something which comes from God's grace and which could never have been achieved or attained or possessed by a man's own effort.

It is Rom. 6.23 which gives the essential meaning of the word. There two words are contrasted with each other. The 'wages' of sin is death. The word used is *opsōnia*, which literally means 'money to buy cooked meat' and which is the regular word for 'a soldier's pay'. That is to say, if we had got the pay we earned it would have been death. The 'gift' of God is eternal life. The word is *charisma*. Now *charisma* also is a military word. When an emperor came to the throne, or when he was celebrating his birthday, he gave his troops a *donativum* or *charisma*, which was a free grant of money, a free gift. They had not earned it as they had their *opsōnia*; they got it unearned out of the goodness of the emperor's heart.

So then what we have earned, our *opsōnia*, would be death. All that we have is *charisma*, God's free gift. All is from God. Every grace with which life is adorned, the grace which covers every sin, every natural endowment we possess, every gift which we can lay at the service of the Church, any office we may hold, every time we have been through something which threatened our bodies or our souls—God gave it, God did it, it is God's *charisma*, all is of God.

> 'And every virtue we possess,
> And every victory won,
> And every thought of holiness
> Are His alone.'

DIATHĒKĒ

MAN AND GOD

THE word *diathēkē* is the word which is translated 'covenant'. It is one of the commonest of all words in the Greek translation of the OT, and it is also a great NT word. It is a word which has a certain problem attached to it, and the solution to that problem will show us that in the word there is a whole theology and a complete view of the relationship between God and man.

In its ordinary, non-theological usage a 'covenant' means 'an agreement entered into between two people'. It is occasionally so used in the OT, e.g. of the 'league' the Gibeonites wished to make with Joshua (Josh. 9.6), of the 'league' with the inhabitants of Canaan which is forbidden (Judg. 2.2), of the 'covenant' between David and Jonathan (I Sam. 23.18).

But far more commonly it is used of the relationship entered into between God and man. It is so used of God's new agreement with man after the flood (Gen. 9.12-17). It is specially used of God's agreement with Abraham (Gen. 17.4-9). And it is used everywhere of the relationship and the agreement between the people of Israel and God (Deut. 4.13, 23). It is uniquely the word which is used to describe 'the relationship, the agreement' between God and the people of God.

In the NT the old usages survive. The covenant with Abraham is still remembered (Acts 7.8). The covenant with the people of Israel is still stressed (Acts 3.25; Rom. 9.4). But very specially it is used of that new relationship between man and God which was made possible by the life and death of Jesus (Matt. 26.28; Mark 14.24; Luke 22.20; II Cor. 3.6). In the NT it is a characteristic word of the letter to the Hebrews to describe this new and better relationship between God and man (Heb. 7.22; 8.6, 9, 10; 12.24; 13.20).

So far everything is straightforward, but the real problem is this—the normal Greek word for a covenant between two people is *sunthēkē*, which is the word everywhere used for a marriage covenant, or an agreement between persons or states. In all normal Greek in all ages *diathēkē* means, not a 'covenant', but a 'will'. *Kata diathēkēn* is the regular term for 'according to the terms of the will'. In a papyrus a testator leaves houses and gardens in accordance with the dispositions (*diathēkas*) which are deposited in the temple of Aphrodite, with Eunomides the governor, and with Ctesiphon the lawyer. Why should the NT never use *sunthēkē* and always *diathēkē*?

The reason is this. *Sunthēkē* always describes 'an agreement made on equal terms', an agreement which either party can alter. But the word 'covenant' means something different. God and man do not meet on equal terms; it means that God, of His own choice and in His free grace, offered man this relationship, which man cannot alter or change or annul, but which he can only accept or refuse. Now the supreme example of such an agreement is 'a will'. The conditions of a will are not made on equal terms. They are made by one person and accepted by the other, who cannot alter them and who could not have made them.

Our relationship with God is not something into which we entered in our own right and on our own terms; it is something given to us solely and completely on the initiative and in the grace of God. Philo says, 'A covenant is a symbol of gracc which God sets between Himself *who extends the boon and man who receives it*.' 'It is fitting for *God to give and for a wise man to receive*.'

The very word 'covenant', *diathēkē*, is a word which in itself sums up our 'debt' and our 'duty' to God. We are in 'debt' because our new relationship to God is due to the approach of God and to nothing that we could ever have done. We have a 'duty' because we have to accept God's conditions of love and faith and obedience, and we cannot alter them. The very word shows that we can never meet God on equal terms, but only on terms of submission and of gratitudc.

Samuel Rutherfurd drew up his own catechism and in it he writes, 'What moved God to make the covenant of grace?' And he answers, 'His own free mercy and grace, for when He made it we were like forlorn bastards and half-dead foundlings that were cast out in the open field to die in their own blood (that actually happened to unwanted children in Rutherfurd's day) when our Lord came by and made a covenant with us.' The very word *diathēkē* has in it the inescapable truth that 'all is of God'.

EILIKRINĒS AND EILIKRINEIA

THE PERFECT PURITY

Eilikrinēs and *eilikrineia*—the first is the adjective and the second is the noun—are two most interesting words. *Eilikrinēs* occurs in Phil. 1.10, where the AV translates it 'sincere', the American RSV 'pure', and Moffatt 'transparent'; it also occurs in II Pet. 3.1, where both the AV and Moffatt translate it 'pure', and the American RSV 'sincere'. *Eilikrineia*, the noun, occurs in I Cor. 5.8, II Cor. 1.12 and II Cor. 2.17. The regular translation of all the versions is 'sincerity', with the one exception that Moffatt in the first example translates it 'innocence'.

Neither the noun nor the adjective is very common in classical Greek. In classical Greek *eilikrinēs* has two characteristic usages. First it means 'unmixed, without alloy, pure'. For instance, fire, the purest thing of all, is said to be *eilikrinēs*. It is used of a 'total' eclipse of the sun. Second, it is used as we use the words 'pure' and 'sheer'. For instance it is used of 'pure' intellect, or 'sheer', 'unrelieved' evil.

In the papyri neither is common. A suppliant appeals to the *eilikrineia* of an official, where the word must mean 'probity, fairness, justice'.

The etymology and derivation of these words in Greek has always been doubtful. There are two suggestions.

(i) They may be derived from a Greek word *eilein* which means 'to shake to and fro in a sieve' until the last particle of foreign matter is extracted and the substance is left absolutely pure. So then these words describe a purity which is 'sifted'. They describe the character which has been so cleansed and purified by the grace of God that there is no evil admixture left.

(ii) They may be derived from a combination of two Greek words, *heilē*, which means 'the sunlight', and *krinein*, which means 'to judge'. They would, in that case, describe something which can stand the judgment of the sunlight, something which even when it is held up to the clear light of the sun reveals no faults and flaws. There is a vivid picture here. In the eastern bazaars the shops were small and dark and shadowed. An article, say a piece of pottery or glassware or cloth, might look all right in the dim recesses of the trader's booth; but the wiser buyer would take it out into the street and hold it up and submit it to the judgment of the sunlight; and many a time the clear rays of the sun would reveal faults and flaws that would never have been noticed in the shadows of the shop. Theopylact must have been thinking of that when he spoke of '*eilikrineia*, purity, of mind and guilelessness which have nothing concealed in the shadows and nothing lurking beneath the surface'.

The question that this word asks is, Could our inmost thoughts stand being brought out into the full light of day? Could our inmost motives stand being dragged out into the full glare of revealing light? To put the matter at its highest, Could the inmost thoughts of our minds and motions of our heart stand the scrutiny of the light of the God's eye?

The Christian purity is a purity which is sifted until the last admixture of evil is gone, a purity which has nothing to conceal and whose inmost thoughts and desires will bear the full glare of the light of day.

EKKLĒSIA

THE CHURCH OF GOD

Ekklēsia is the NT word for 'church', and is, therefore, one of the most important of all NT words. Like so many NT words it has a double background.

(i) *Ekklēsia* has a Greek background. In the great classical days in Athens the *ekklēsia* was the convened assembly of the people. It consisted of all the citizens of the city who had not lost their civic rights. Apart from the fact that its decisions must conform to the laws of the State, its powers were to all intents and purposes unlimited. It elected and dismissed magistrates and directed the policy of the city. It declared war, made peace, contracted treaties and arranged alliances. It elected generals and other military officers. It assigned troops to different campaigns and dispatched them from the city. It was ultimately responsible for the conduct of all military operations. It raised and allocated funds. Two things are interesting to note. First, all its meetings began with prayer and sacrifice. Second, it was a true democracy. Its two great watchwords were 'equality' (*isonomia*) and 'freedom' (*eleutheria*). It was an assembly where everyone had an equal right and an equal duty to take part. When a case involving the right of any private citizen was before it—as in the case of ostracism or banishment—at least 6,000 citizens must be present. In the wider Greek world *ekklēsia* came to mean any duly convened assembly of citizens. It is interesting to note that the Roman world did not even try to translate the word *ekklēsia*; it simply transliterated it into *ecclesia* and used it in the same way. There is an interesting bilingual inscription found in Athens (dated A.D. 103-4). It can be read against the background of Acts 18. A certain Caius Vibius Salutaris had presented to the city an image of Diana and other images. The inscription lays it down that they are to be set up on their pedestals at every *ekklēsia* of the city in the theatre. To Greek and Roman alike the word was familiar in the sense of a convened assembly. So, then, when we look at it against this background, as Deissmann puts it, the Church was God's assembly, God's muster, and the convener is God.

(ii) *Ekklēsia* has a Hebrew background. In the Septuagint it translates the Hebrew word *qahal*, which again comes from a root which means 'to summon'. It is regularly used for the 'assembly' or the 'congregation' of the people of Israel. In Deut. 18.16; Judg. 20.2, it is translated 'assembly'; and in I Kings 8.14; Lev. 10.17; Num. 1.16, it is translated 'congregation'. It is very common in the Septuagint, occurring over 70 times. In the Hebrew sense it, therefore, means God's people called together by God, in order to listen to or to act for God. In a certain sense the word 'congregation' loses a certain amount of the essential meaning. A 'congregation' is a company of people 'who have come together'; a *quahal* or an *ekklēsia* is a body of people 'who have been called together'. The two original words, Hebrew and Greek, put all the emphasis on the action of God.

F. J. A. Hort rightly points out that originally the word does not mean, as is so often stated, a body of people who have been 'picked out' from the world. It has not in it that exclusive sense. It means a body of people who have been 'summoned out' of their homes to come and meet with God; and both in its original Greek and Hebrew usages, that sense was not exclusive but inclusive. The summons was not to any selected few; it was a summons from the State to every man to come and to shoulder his responsibilities; it was a summons from God to every man to come and to listen to and to act on the word of God.

In essence, therefore, the Church, the *ekklēsia*, is a body of people, not so much assembling because they have chosen to come together, but assembling because God has called them to Himself; not so much assembling to share their own thoughts and opinions, but assembling to listen to the voice of God.

In the NT *ekklēsia* can be used in three different ways. (i) It means 'the universal Church' (I Cor. 10.32; 12.28; Phil.

3.6). (ii) It means 'A particular local Church' (Rom. 16.1; I Cor. 1.2; Gal. 1.2). (iii) It means 'the actual assembly' of the believers in any place, met together for worship (I Cor. 11.18; 14.19; 14.23). In this matter it seems that Paul's thought developed. In his very early letters he thought rather of the individual congregations. So, for instance, he speaks of the '*ekklēsia* of the Thessalonians' (I Thess. 1.1; II Thess. 1.2). But later he speaks of the '*ekklēsia* of God which is at Corinth' (I Cor. 1.2). Paul came to think of the Church, not in terms of separate congregations, but in terms of one great universal Church of which each congregation was a part. Sir William Ramsay saw in the Roman Empire a foreshadowing of this which may well have affected the thought of Paul. Any group of Roman citizens, meeting anywhere throughout the world, was a *conventus civium Romanorum*, 'an assembly of Roman citizens'. Wherever they might be meeting they were part of the great conception of Rome. They had no meaning apart from Rome; they were part of a great unity. And any citizen coming into that town was automatically and without introduction a member of the group. Such a group might be separated from Rome in space, but in spirit they were part of it. That is precisely the Pauline conception of the Church. A man must be a member of a local congregation, within a certain given communion; but if his thought stops there he is far away from the true conception of the Church.

The Church is the universal whole of which his little congregation forms a part, and the important thing is, not that he is a member of such and such a congregation, or even of such and such a communion, but that he is a member of the Church of God. To take an army parallel—a man might be proud to be a soldier in the Argyll and Sutherland Highlanders; but that regiment was part of the Eighth Army, and that would bring to him an even greater pride; and that army was part of the army of his native country, which ought to be his greatest pride of all. It is good to be proud of a congregation; it is good to remember the tradition of a denomination. It is best of all to be conscious of being a member of the Church of God.

In the NT the Church is set before us in three relationships.

(i) It is sometimes—not often—described in human terms. So, for instance, Paul speaks of the Church of the Thessalonians (I Thess. 1.1; II Thess. 1.2). In a sense the Church is composed of men and belongs to men; men are the bricks out of which the edifice of the Church is built. It is worth noting that in all the NT the word Church is never used to describe a 'building'. It always describes a body of men and women who have given their hearts to God.

(ii) Far more frequently it is described in divine terms. By far the commonest description is the 'Church of God' (I Cor. 1.2; II Cor. 1.1; Gal. 1.13; I Thess. 2.14; I Tim. 3.5, 15). The Church belongs to God and comes from God. Had there been no such thing as the love of God there would have been no such thing as a Church; and unless God was a self-communicating God there would be no message and no help in the Church.

(iii) Sometimes the Church is described as the Church of Christ. (*a*) In this connection Christ is the head of the Church (Eph. 5.23, 24). It ought to be according to the mind and thought and will of Christ that the Church lives and moves. (*b*) The Church is the body of Christ (Col. 1.24). It is through the Church that Jesus Christ acts. It must be hands to work for Him, feet to run upon His errands, a voice to speak for Him. An Indian described the Church as 'the Church which carries on the life of Christ'.

One last point is to be noted. In NT times the Church had no buildings. Christians met in any house which had a room large enough to accommodate them. These gatherings were called 'house-churches' (Rom. 16.5; I Cor. 16.19; Col. 4.15; Philem. 2). Every home ought to be in a real sense a Church. Jesus is Lord of the dinner table as He is Lord of the Communion table. And it will always be true that they pray best together who first pray alone.

EPIEIKĒS AND EPIEIKEIA

MORE THAN JUSTICE

WE will not begin with a translation of *epieikēs* for the very good reason that it is extremely difficult to produce one. The adjective *epieikēs* occurs in the NT five times, and the noun *epieikeia* twice. On these seven occasions Moffatt uses six different translations. In Phil. 4.5, where the neuter of the adjective is used as a noun, he translates it 'forbearance'; in I Tim. 3.3, 'lenient'; in Tit. 3.2, 'conciliatory'; in Jas. 3.17, 'forbearing'; and in I Pet. 2.18, 'reasonable'. The two occurrences of the noun are in Acts 24.4, and II Cor. 10.1, which Moffatt respectively translates 'courtesy' and 'consideration'. The American RSV is more consistent. In the occurrences of the adjective, except in the first case, where it also translates 'forbearance', it consistently translates by the word 'gentle'; and in the two occurrences of the noun it uses 'kindness' in the first and 'gentleness' in the second.

Long before the NT used it, this word had a great record in Greek ethical writings. Trench sums up the meaning that is behind it when he says that it expresses that 'moderation which recognizes the impossibility that cleaves to formal law'. He says that it is the word which recognizes that there are occasions when a 'legal' right can become a 'moral' wrong. Aristotle discussed *epieikeia* in the *Nicomachean Ethics*. He says that *epieikeia* is that which is just and sometimes that which is better than justice (*Eth. Nic.* v. 10.6). He says that *epieikeia* is that which corrects the law when the law is deficient because of its generality. He compares the man who is *epieikēs* with the man who is *akribodikaios*. The man who is *akribodikaios* is the man who stands up for the last tittle of his legal rights; but the man who is *epieikēs* knows that there are times when a thing may be legally completely justified and yet morally completely wrong. The man who is *epieikēs* knows when to relax the law under the compulsion of a force that is higher and greater than law. He knows the time when to stand on his rights would unquestionably be legal, and would just as unquestionably be completely unchristian.

The basic and the fundamental thing about *epieikeia* is that it goes back to God. If God stood on His rights, if God applied to us nothing but the rigid standards of law, where would we be? God is the supreme example of one who is *epieikēs* and who deals with others with *epieikeia*.

It may be hard to translate this word, but it is not hard to see the clamant need of the quality which it describes. We live in a society where men insist on standing on their legal rights, where they will do only what they are compelled to do, and where they desire to make others do all that they can compel them to do. Again and again we have seen congregations torn by strife and reduced to tragic unhappiness because men and women, committees and courts stood on the letter of the law. When a congregation's governing body meets with a copy of its Church's book of laws prominently displayed on the chairman's table trouble is never far away. A new world would arise in society and in the Church if men ceased to base their actions on law and on legal rights and prayed to God to give them *epieikeia*.

ERITHEIA

THE WRONG KIND OF AMBITION

Eritheia is a word whose meaning degenerated, and the story of its degeneration is in itself a grim commentary on human nature. In the NT it is used seven times, and always of a fault which ruins Church work. In Rom. 2.8 it is used to describe those who are 'contentious'; in II Cor. 12.20 it occurs amid a list of faults which are ruining the Church at Corinth, and in Gal. 5.20 it is one of the works of the flesh, and in both cases the AV translates it 'strife'; in Phil. 1.16 and 2.3 it is used to describe the wrong motive for preaching and the wrong spirit in which to live; the AV translates it, in the first case, 'contention', and in the second, 'strife'; it is twice used in James (3.14; 3.16), where it is a characteristic of the wisdom which is not from above and where the AV translates it 'envying'.

Now the interesting thing about this word is that, with these cases before us, we would very naturally and almost inevitably derive it from *eris*, which is the word for 'strife'; but that is not its derivation at all. *Erithos* originally meant 'a day labourer'; the word was specially connected with 'spinners' and 'weavers', and the popular derivation was from *erion*, which means 'wool'. *Eritheia* therefore began by being a perfectly respectable word with the meaning 'labour for wages'. It then begins to degenerate. It began to mean that kind of work which is done for motives of pay and for nothing else; that kind of work which has no motive of service whatever and which has only one question—What do I get out of it? It therefore went on to mean 'canvassing and intriguing for public office'. It was the characteristic of the man who sought public office, not for any service he could render the State, but simply and solely for his own honour and glory and for his own profit. It then acquired two other meanings. First, it came to be used of 'party squabbles', of the jockeying for position and the intriguing for place and power which is so often characteristic of both secular and ecclesiastical politics. Second, it ended up by meaning 'selfish ambition', the ambition which has no conception of service and whose only aims are profit and power.

It is extremely interesting to see how the NT uses it. By far its greater number of uses occur in Paul, and no one knew the inside of the Early Church better than Paul did. It was the fault which could so easily wreck a Church. It was the fault which nearly wrecked the Church of God at Corinth by splitting it into sects and factions who were more concerned with their own supremacy than the supremacy of Christ. In Philippi it had actually become the moving motive of certain preachers. They were eager rather to show their own greatness than the greatness of Christ. Long ago Denney bitingly said that no preacher can show at one and the same time that he is clever and that Christ is wonderful. It was characteristic in Paul of the works of the flesh and in James of the earthly and sensual wisdom. It is the characteristic of the man who applies earthly and human standards to everything, and who assesses things by the measuring rod of personal prestige and personal success.

It is an illuminating light on human nature that the word which began by describing the work that a man does for an honest day's pay came in the end to describe the work which is done for pay and pay alone. It is a warning to our own generation, for most of our troubles to-day are not basically economic troubles; they spring rather from the spirit which asks, always, What can I get out of life? and, never, What can I put into life?

EUAGGELION

THE GOOD NEWS

THE word *euaggelion* means 'gospel' or 'good news', and when we come to study it we are of necessity at the very heart and centre of the Christian faith. The word *euaggelion* is so specifically and characteristically a Christian word that it has not a long history outside the NT. In classical Greek it has three meanings. (i) Originally it meant 'the reward given to a messenger for bringing good tidings'. It is so used in the Septuagint in II Sam. 4.10. (ii) It went on to mean 'the sacrifices made to the gods when such good tidings were received'. (iii) Not in classical Greek at all, but in late hellenistic Greek it comes to mean 'the good tidings themselves'. In the Septuagint it is used for the good tidings of 'victory' (I Sam. 31.9), the good tidings of 'the birth of a child' (Jer. 20.15), and sometimes simply of tidings of any kind.

In the Septuagint it has two usages which are faint foretastes of its NT use. (i) In the Psalms the corresponding verb is used of telling forth the righteousness and the saving power of God (Ps. 40.10; 96.2). (ii) In Isaiah it is used of the glad tidings of the coming of God's anointed one to His people (Isa. 40.9; 52.7). In the papyri both noun and verb are very rare. The verb (*euaggelizesthai*) is used of a slave coming with news of a general's victory, and the noun (*euaggelion*) is used in an inscription which says that the birthday of the Roman Emperor Augustus was the beginning of good tidings for the world. But it is when we come to the NT that *euaggelion* becomes a tremendous word.

(i) It is the word which is the summation of the whole Christian message (Mark 1.1; I Cor. 15.1). The Kingdom which Jesus preached is 'good news' (Matt. 4.23; 9.35; 24.14). The proof of the centrality of this word in the Christian message can be seen from the fact that *euaggelion* occurs 72 times in the NT and of these 72 instances 54 are in Paul's letters. To the greatest of the Christian missionaries Christianity was essentially 'good news'. There is an implicit contrast here. The preaching of John the Baptist with its consuming fire, its winnowing fan, its axe laid to the root of the tree is the reverse of good news. It is tidings of disaster, but the whole essence of the message of Jesus is 'good news of God'.

(ii) Sometimes the *euaggelion* is spoken of as the *euaggelion* 'of God' (Mark 1.14; I Thess. 2.2, 8, 9). It is good news of God in two senses. (*a*) It showed to men a God the like of whom they had never dreamed, a God whose heart was love. (*b*) It was good news 'sent by God'. Behind the whole process of salvation is God. It is always wrong to think of an angry God and a gentle Christ, to think that what Jesus did changed the attitude of God to men. It was because God so loved the world that He sent His Son. The good news is *of* God and *from* God.

(iii) Sometimes *euaggelion* is spoken of as the *euaggelion* of 'Jesus Christ' (Mark 1.1; II Cor. 4.4; 9.13; 10.14). It is the good news of Jesus Christ in two senses. (*a*) Jesus 'brought' it to men. Without Him they would never have known it. (*b*) Jesus 'embodied' it to men. He did not only *tell* men what God was like, He *showed* them the Father.

(iv) Sometimes Paul uses the expression 'my' or 'our'

euaggelion (II Cor. 4.3; I Thess. 1.5; II Thess. 2.14). The good news comes from God, and belongs to God. It is brought by Jesus and belongs to Jesus. But, for all that, a man must 'appropriate' it until it belongs to him. He must pass it through his mind and receive it into his heart until it is utterly and inalienably his.

(v) The *euaggelion* is for all men (Mark 13.10; 16.15; Acts 15.7). The Jews had always believed that in God's economy there was a most favoured nation clause. But the gospel of Christ is the gospel without boundaries. The good news is good news for all.

Let us go on to see certain things about this *euaggelion*, this 'good news' in regard to man.

(i) The *euaggelion* is not a human discovery, it is 'a revelation from God'. The fact that God is as Jesus showed Him to be is not something which a man could have discovered by intellectual processes. Man does not discover God. *God reveals Himself* (Gal. 1.11, 12).

(ii) The *euaggelion* is something in which a man must 'believe' (Mark 1.15). The whole of Christianity consists in living life in the unalterable conviction that the good news that Jesus brought about God is true.

(iii) The *euaggelion* is something which he who knows must 'proclaim to others' (Rom. 15.19; I Cor. 9.14, 18; II Cor. 10.14; 11.7; Gal. 2.2). When a man has found the good news, he has not truly found it until he wishes to share it with others. A missionary tells of an Indian who had been hostile to Christianity and who was converted to it. He got himself a Bible. He got used to reading it, and, as he read, he would come upon a passage which spoke to his heart, and with his finger in the place, he would rush out into the road and stop each passer-by, crying out, 'Have you heard about this?' No Christian can keep the good news to himself. Every Christian is a missionary.

(iv) That task of spreading the *euaggelion* is not something which a man chooses, but something which is 'entrusted' to him and 'laid upon' him (I Thess. 2.4; I Cor. 9.16). It is most literally 'for God's sake' that he must pass on the good news, which he himself has received.

(v) The *euaggelion* is something for which a man must

'risk everything' (Mark 8.35; 10.29; Rom. 1.16; I Cor. 9.23). He must be prepared to stake everything on the certainty that the man who obeys God's commandments will find God's promises true.

(vi) The *euaggelion* is something which a man can 'serve' (Rom. 1.1; 15.16; Phil. 1.12; 2.22; 4.3; I Thess. 3.2). The reception of the good news points at one and the same time 'to privilege and to duty'. A man must give his life to that which gave him life.

(vii) The *euaggelion* is something which a man can 'defend' (Phil. 1.7, 17). By his life and words and conduct and action he must at every moment be 'a defender of the faith'.

(viii) The *euaggelion* is something which a man can 'hinder' (I Cor. 9.12). It is the awe-inspiring responsibility of the Christian life that every one of us can make others think less or more of the Christian faith.

(ix) The *euaggelion* is something which a man can 'miss' or 'refuse' (Rom. 2.16; 10.16; II Thess. 1.7, 8; I Pet. 4.17). To the end of the day a man's will is free. It is the characteristic of love that love can only offer and can never coerce. A man can spurn the offer of God or he can completely disregard it. He can live life as if the good news did not exist, but he does so at the peril of his immortal soul.

(x) The *euaggelion* is something which a man can 'twist' and 'distort' (II Cor. 11.4; Gal. 1.6, 7). There is such a thing as preaching what Paul called 'another gospel'. When a man begins to believe in or to seek to propagate Christianity as he would like it to be instead of as God proclaims it is, he cannot do other than preach 'another gospel'. It is only after we have listened to God that we can speak to men. The danger is that we tell God instead of listening to God telling us.

As we study this word *euaggelion* and as we trace it through the NT we begin to see that it involves and includes certain things.

(i) The *euaggelion* is 'the good news of truth' (Gal. 2.5, 14; Col. 1.5). With the coming of Jesus Christ the time of guesses about God is ended and the time of certainty begun.

With His coming the time of groping after the meaning and the method of life is closed and the time of certainty is here. Christianity was never meant to present men with a series of problems but with an armoury of certainties.

(ii) The *euaggelion* is 'the good news of hope' (Col. 2.23). The man who tries to live life with only the materials which human effort can bring to it cannot do other than despair of himself and despair of the world. John Buchan defined an atheist as 'a man with no invisible means of support'. When a man realizes what the good news means he is filled with hope for himself and for the world.

(iii) The *euaggelion* is 'the good news of peace' (Eph. 6.15). So long as a man tries to live life alone he is inevitably a split personality. As Studdert-Kennedy said, 'Part of him comes from heaven, and part of him comes from earth.' The good news tells us that victory comes from surrender, from the death of self and the rising to life of Christ within us. The good news brings to men the possibility of a fully integrated personality where the old unhappy tensions are ended.

(iv) The *euaggelion* is 'the good news of God's promise' (Eph. 3.6). The characteristic of the pagan gods, and even of God as the OT knew Him, was that He was a God of threats. Jesus brought the good news which told not of the God of the threat, but the God of the promise. That by no means removes all obligations from life, for a promise brings its obligation just as much as a threat does, but the obligation becomes the obligation to answer to love and not to cower before vengeance.

(v) The *euaggelion* is 'the good news of immortality" (II Tim. 1.10). In face of death the pagan sorrowed and feared as one who had no hope (I Thess. 4.13). One of the saddest of papyrus letters is a letter from a mother to a mother and father whose little child has died. 'Irene to Taonnophris and Philo, good comfort. I was as sorry and wept over the departed one as I wept for Didymus. All things that were fitting I did. . . . But all the same in the face of such things *there is nothing that anyone can do.*' That was the pagan outlook in the face of death. But the good news brings the certainty that death is not the end but the beginning of life, not the departure into annihilation but the departure to be for ever with God.

(vi) The *euaggelion* is 'good news of the risen Christ' (I Cor. 15.1 ff.; II Tim. 2.8). The good news which Christianity brings is that we do not worship a dead hero, but we live with a living presence. We are not left with only a pattern to copy and an example to follow, we are left with a constant companion of our way. Our faith is not a faith in a figure in a book who lived and died, but in one who rose from death and who is alive forever more.

(vii) The *euaggelion* is 'good news of salvation' (Eph. 1.13). It is news of that power which wins us forgiveness for past sin, liberation from present sin, strength for the future to conquer sin. It is good news of victory.

EXALEIPHEIN

THE MERCY WHICH WIPES OUT SIN

THE word *exaleiphein* occurs only five times in the NT, but one, at least, of its uses is of the greatest interest and importance. In classical Greek the word begins by meaning 'to wash over'. It is used, for instance, of 'whitewashing' the wall of a house. It is used of warriors 'painting' their bodies with war paint. Herodotus (7.39) tells us that the Ethiopians painted (*exaleiphein*) their bodies, half with chalk and half with vermilion, before they went into battle. It is used of 'anointing' with oil. It goes on to mean 'to wipe out or to obliterate'. It is so used of 'wiping out' a memory of an experience from one's remembrance or one's mind; of 'cancelling' a vote or 'annulling' a law; of 'cancelling' a charge or a debt or of 'striking a man's name off a roll' or list; of 'wiping a family completely out of existence'.

In the contemporary papyri it retains all its meanings. A man writes to his friend, 'I could not read your letter because it had been obliterated (*exaleiphein*).' Always it has this meaning of wiping something out as you would with a sponge.

In the NT it is twice used literally. In Rev. 7.17 and 21.4 it is used of 'wiping away' the tear from every eye. In Rev. 3.5 it is used for 'wiping out' a man's name from a roll. In Acts 3.19 it is used of wiping out sin. Repent, the AV translates it, that your sins may be 'blotted out'. But the remaining instance is the one which is of supreme interest. In Col. 2.14 Paul speaks of Jesus 'blotting out the handwriting of ordinances that was against us'. Now the word that Paul uses for handwriting is *cheirographos*. Literally it means a 'holograph'. It goes on to mean a 'signature' and then a 'written agreement'. But it came to mean technically 'a written agreement acknowledging a debt', a 'certificate of debt', a 'bond'. In the papyri, a men writes to his friend, 'If you can, please get on to Dioscurus and exact from him his *bond*.' A *cheirographos* was a document which acknowledged a debt that had to be paid. It was that that Jesus wiped out for us. Let us remember the literal meaning of *exaleiphein*. Literally it means 'to wipe out'. In NT times documents were written on papyrus. The ink was made of soot, mixed with gum and diluted with water. The characteristic of this ink is that it has no acid in it and therefore does not bite into the paper. It will last a very long time and will retain its colour, but if, soon after it is written, a wet sponge was passed over the surface of the papyrus, the writing could be sponged off as completely as writing might be sponged from a slate. Now the interesting thing is this—a commoner word for cancelling a certificate of debt was *chiazein*. *Chiazein* means to write the Greek letter *chi*, which was the same shape as a capital X, right across the document. So, after a trial in Egypt, the governor gives orders that a bond should be cancelled (*chiazesthai*), that is, 'crossed out'. But Paul does not say that Jesus Christ 'crossed out' (*chiazein*) the record of our debt; he says that He 'wiped it out' (*exalephein*). If you 'cross a thing out', beneath the cross, the record still remains visible for anyone to read, but if you 'wipe it out' the record is gone, obliterated for ever. It is as if God, for Jesus' sake, not only 'crossed out' our debt, but 'wiped it out'. There is many a man who can forgive, but who never really forgets the injury that was done to him; but God not only forgives but wipes out the very memory of the debt. There is a kind of forgiveness which forgives but still holds the memory against the sinner; but God's forgiveness is that surpreme forgiveness which can forgive and forget.

HAMARTIA AND HAMARTANEIN

THE FAILURE WHICH IS SIN

Hamartia is the commonest NT noun for 'sin'; it occurs in Paul's letters 60 times; and *hamartanein* is the usual verb for 'to sin'. In classical Greek these words had not nearly so serious a meaning as in NT Greek. In classical Greek *hamartia* has as its basic meaning the idea of 'failure'. *Hamartanein* began by meaning 'to miss the mark' as when a spear is thrown at a target. It can be used for missing a road, for failure in one's plan or hope or purpose. In classical Greek these words are always connected with some kind of negative failure rather than with some kind of positive transgression, but in the NT they come to describe something which is very much more serious.

It is to be noted that in the NT *hamartia* does not describe a definite act of sin; it describes the state of sin, from which acts of sin come. In fact in Paul sin becomes almost personalized until sin could be spelled with a capital letter, and could be thought of as malignant, personal power which has man in its grasp.

Let us then see what the NT teaches about *hamartia*.

(i) *Hamartia*, 'sin', is 'universal' (Rom. 3.23; 7.14; Gal. 3.22; I John 1.8). Sin is not like a disease which some men contract and some escape. It is something in which every single human being is involved and of which every human being is guilty. Sin is not simply a sporadic and spasmodic outbreak; it is the universal state of man.

(ii) *Hamartia*, 'sin', is 'a power which has man in its grasp'. Here the words which are used are very interesting and significant. Man is *huph' hamartian*. Literally that means 'under sin'. But this preposition *hupo* with the accusative case, as here, is used to mean 'in dependence on, in subjection to, under the control of'. A minor, for instance, is 'under his father'; an army is 'under its commander'; so we are 'under, in the power of, in the control of sin' (Gal. 3.22; Rom. 3.9). So certain words are used of sin. Sin is said 'to rule over (*basileuein*) men' (Rom. 5.21). *Basileus* is the Greek for 'a king'. Sin is the ruler of men. Sin is said 'to lord it over us' (*kurieuein*) (Rom. 6.14). *Kurios* is the Greek for 'lord', and the word has the flavour of absolute 'possession' and 'domination'. Sin is said 'to take us captive' (*aichmalōtizein*) (Rom. 7.23). The word is the word which is used for taking a prisoner in war. Sin is said 'to dwell within man' (*oikein, enoikein*) (Rom. 7.17, 20). So basic is the hold of sin over man that sin is not merely an external power which exercises sway over a man; it has got into the very fibre and centre and heart of his being until it occupies him, as an enemy occupies an occupied country. The result is that we can be said 'to be the slaves of sin' (*doulos, douleuein*) (John 8.34; Rom. 6.17, 20; Rom. 6.6). It is to be remembered that the power of the master over the slave was absolute. There was no part of life, no moment of time, no activity which was the personal property of the slave. He belonged to his master in the most total way. So man is totally under the domination of sin.

In Paul there is the closest connection between 'law' and 'sin', between *nomos* and *hamartia*.

(i) The law 'teaches what sin is' (Rom. 3.20). It may be said in one sense that the law creates sin (Rom. 5.13). Sin is not sin until it is defined. Until sin is defined a man cannot know what sin is; and until there is a law of sin a man cannot be guilty of sin. To take an analogy—a city street may be for long unrestricted and a motorist may be able to drive his car along it in either direction; then a law is made which makes that street a one-way street. It then becomes a breach of the law to drive along that street in the wrong direction. The laying down of that law has created a new breach of the law. The law has both defined and created sin. If there were no law there would be no sin.

(ii) But 'the law creates sin', as Paul sees it, in another sense. Once a thing is forbidden it somehow or other acquires a new and a fatal fascination, and the law actually produces the desire to sin (Rom. 7.8-11). There is something in human nature which gives the forbidden thing a double attraction. C. H. Dodd quotes the classic example of that from the *Confessions* of Augustine (2.4-6). 'There was a pear-tree near our vineyard, laden with fruit. One stormy night we rascally youths set out to rob it and to carry our spoils away. We took a huge load of pears—not to feast upon them ourselves, but to throw them to the pigs—though we ate just enough to have the pleasure of forbidden fruit. They were nice pears, but it was not the pears that my wretched soul coveted, for I had plenty better at home. I picked them simply in order to be a thief. The only feast I got was a feast of iniquity, and that I enjoyed to the full. What was it I loved in that theft? Was it the pleasure of acting against the law, in order that I, a prisoner under rules, might have a maimed counterfeit of freedom, by doing with impunity what was forbidden, with a dim similitude of omnipotence?' And then Dr. Dodd comments: 'That is to say that the desire to steal was aroused simply by the prohibition of stealing.' It is precisely here that the weakness of the law in regard to sin emerges. Law has two defects. First, it can define sin but it cannot cure it. It is like a doctor who can diagnose a disease but who is helpless to eradicate or even arrest it. Second, it is the odd and fatal fact that simply by forbidding a thing the law makes that thing attractive. There is an inextricable connection between *hamartia* and *nomos*, 'sin' and 'law'.

There are certain inevitable consequences of sin.

(i) Sin results in a certain 'hardening' of the heart. The word used for hardening is *sklērunein* (Heb. 3.13). The adjective *sklēros* can be used, for instance, of a stone which is specially hard for masons to work; it can be used metaphorically of a king who is inhuman and hard in his treatment of his subjects. Sin hardens the heart. In Phil. 1.9 Paul prays that the Philippians may abound in what he calls *aisthēsis,* which is 'sensitive perception'. It is the quality of heart and mind which is sensitive to that which is wrong. It is the experience of life that the first time a man commits a wrong action he does so with a kind of shuddering reluctance; if he does it twice he does it more easily; if he goes on doing it he will end by doing it without thinking at all. His sensitiveness to sin is gone; his heart is hardened. It is indeed true that the most awful thing about sin is exactly its power to beget sin.

(ii) Sin results in 'death' (Rom. 5.12, 21; 6.16; 6.23; Jas. 1.15). This is doubly so. It was Paul's belief that it was because of Adam's sin that death entered into the world. Sin is that which wrecked and ruined the life that God had planned for man. But it is also true that death results in the death of the soul. Physical death and spiritual death are to Paul both the result of sin.

One of the best ways of discovering the real meeaning of any word is to examine the company it keeps. A word's meaning, and its inward flavour, will best be found by examining the words in whose company it is usually found. Let us, then, examine the words with which *hamartia* is found in the NT.

(i) *Hamartia* is connected with *blasphēmia* (Matt. 12.31). The basic meaning of *blasphēmia* is insult. Sin is then 'an insult' to God. It insults God by flouting His commandments, by putting self in the place which He ought to occupy, and above all, by grieving His love.

(ii) *Hamartia* is connected with *apatē* (Heb. 3.13). *Apatē* is 'deceit'. Sin is always a deceitful thing, in that it promises to do that which it cannot do. Sin is always a lie. Any man who sins, who does the forbidden thing or who takes the forbidden thing, does so because he thinks that he will be happier for doing or taking that thing. Sin deceives him into thinking so. But the plain fact of experience that an act or a possession which is the result of sin never brought happiness to any man. Long ago, Epicurus, with his strictly utilitarian morality, pointed out that sin can never bring happiness, because, apart from anything else, it leaves a man with the constant fear of being found out.

(iii) *Hamartia* is connected with *epithumia* (Jas. 1.15). *Epithumia* is desire. *Epithumia* was defined by Aristotle as 'reaching after pleasure'. The Stoics added to that definition by saying that it was a reaching after pleasure 'beyond the bounds of reason'. Clement of Alexandria defined *epithumia* as the spirit which 'aims at and reaches after that which will gratify itself'. *Epithumia* always has the notion of desiring that which should not be desired. *Epithumein* is in fact the verb which is used in the Greek version of the tenth commandment, 'Thou shalt not *covet*.' If a man's heart was so cleansed that he never desired the wrong thing he would never sin.

(iv) *Hamartia* is equated with *anomia* (I John 3.4). *Anomia* is 'lawlessness'. Sin is that which every now and then makes a man desire to kick over the traces, to have done with restraints and controls, to do exactly as he likes. *Anomia* is the spirit which makes a man desire to erect his own wishes above his duty to man and his obedience to God. *Anomia* springs basically from the desire to instal self and not God at the centre of life.

(v) *Hamartia* is equated with *adikia* (I John 5.17). *Adikia* is 'injustice, unrighteousness, evil'. It is the opposite of *dikaiosunē*, which means 'justice'. Now *dikaiosunē* may be defined as 'giving both to God and to men that which is their due'. *Adikia*, then, is the spirit which at one and the same time refuses its duty to God and its duty to men. Sin is that which makes a man so worship self that he forgets or refuses to serve God and to serve his fellow-men. It is that which makes him act as if he were the most important person in the universe.

(vi) *Hamartia* is connected with *prosōpolēpsia* (Jas. 2.9). *Prosōpolēpsia* is 'respect of person'. Now respect of persons is the result of applying man's standards instead of God's standards to the world and to life and to people in general. Sin is to accept the world's standards instead of the standards of God, to judge things as men see them instead of as God sees them.

It is time now to turn to the cure of *hamartia*. Let us now look at certain of the words which describe what Jesus Christ does for us in relation to sin.

(i) Jesus 'saves' us from sin (*sōzein*) (Matt. 1.21). We are in the position of people who need to be rescued and that rescue is carried out by Jesus at the cost of His life.

(ii) Our sins are 'wiped out' (*exaleiphein*) (Acts 3.19). Ancient ink had no acid in it. It could be sponged off the surface of vellum or of papyrus when the scribe wanted to use the vellum or the papyrus again. Because of the work of Jesus the record of our sin is obliterated, sponged away.

(iii) Through Jesus we are 'washed from sin' (*apolouein*) (Acts 22.16). There comes a 'cleansing from sin' (*katharismos*) (Heb. 1.3; II Pet. 1.9; I John 1.7). It is as if life was soiled and mired and stained and muddied by sin; and Jesus Christ has the power to cleanse it, as the rain washes clean the city pavements.

(iv) In the mercy of God 'a veil is drawn across our sin' (*epikaluptein*) (Rom. 4.7). The verb *epikaluptein* is used of snow obliterating a pathway; it is used of someone covering his eyes so that he cannot see; it is used of drawing a veil over something. It is as if God in His mercy drew a veil over the sorry record of the past and never looked at it again.

(v) In the mercy of God our sins 'are not reckoned against us' (*logizesthai*) (Rom. 4.8). *Logizesthai* is an accountant's word. It means 'to set down to someone's account'. The idea is that our sins have put us completely and unpayably in God's debt. The balance of the ledger of life is infinitely against us. But God in His mercy wipes out the debit balance which we ourselves could never pay.

(vi) By the work of Jesus we are 'liberated from sin' (*eleutheroun*) (Rom. 6.18, 22; 8.2). We are 'released from sin' (*luein*) (Rev. 1.5). *Eleutheroun* means 'to give someone his freedom'. *Luein* means 'to loose someone from his bonds'. We have already seen how man has become the slave of sin, has got himself into the control of sin. Jesus is the supreme liberator and emancipator. At one and the same time He pays the ransom price which liberates from the past and gives the power which gives freedom for the future.

(vii) The coming of Jesus 'cancelled our sin' (*athetēsis*)

(Heb. 9.26). *Athetēsis* is technical, legal Greek for 'the cancellation of a contract or agreement'. Were the strict letter of the law carried out there could be for man nothing but condemnation. Through Jesus there is a cancellation of the debt we owe.

(viii) Through Jesus 'we are forgiven' (*aphiesthai*). This is the word which is by far the commonest for the forgiveness of sins. It occurs in every stratum of the NT (Matt. 9.2; Mark 2.10; Luke 7.47; Acts 2.38; 10.43; Col. 1.14; I John 2.12). The word *aphiesthai* has a wide variety of meanings, all of which have some suggestion to make. It can be used for releasing a man from some sentence that has already been passed, as, for instance, from exile. It can be used for remitting a charge that has justly been made. It can be used for acquitting a man from a verdict that might have been carried out or from releasing him from an engagement that might have been insisted upon. It can be used of absolving a man from duty that he could have been compelled to carry out. The whole essence of the word is the undeserved release of a man from something that might justly have been inflicted upon him or exacted from him. Through Jesus Christ man is released from the punishment and penalty that God had every right to inflict upon him. It is the word which tells us that God deals with us, not in justice, but in love; that we are dealt with, not according to our deserts, but according to His mercy and His grace in Jesus Christ.

There is no book which has so great a sense of the horror and the awfulness of sin as the NT has, but equally there is no book which is so sure that the cure and the remedy have been found.

HUPOGRAMMOS

THE PERFECT PATTERN

THERE is only one example of the word *hupogrammos* in the NT, but it is an example with a vivid picture behind it. Peter says of Jesus that 'He left us an example (*hupogrammos*) that we should follow in His steps' (I Pet. 2.21).

The word *hupogrammos* is a word which comes from Greek primary education. It is a word which has to do with the way in which Greek boys were taught to write. The common writing material in NT times were *papyrus*, which was a kind of paper made of the pith of the bulrush which grew mainly on the banks of the Nile. It was by no means a cheap material. It was usually manufactured in sheets which measured ten by eight inches. The sheets varied in quality and in price. The cheapest sheets were about fourpence; and the dearest slightly more than a shilling. Obviously papyrus was far too expensive a substance for boys to practise writing on. So, then, the schoolboy's exercise book was usually the wax tablet. The wax tablet was like a very shallow box filled with soft wax. The writing was done with a *stylus* which was pointed at one end and flat at the other. The pointed end was used to write with, and the flat end was used to smooth over the wax, so that it could be used again.

The method by which boys were taught to write is outlined for us in two places. Plato in the *Protagoras* (326 D) tells us that in teaching to write the writing master first drew lines (*hupographein*, which is the verb corresponding to the noun *hupogrammos*) with a stylus for the use of the learner, and then gave him the tablet and made him write as the lines directed. In practice this meant two things. The writing master drew parallel lines to keep the boy's writing straight; and he also wrote at the top of the tablet a line of writing which the boy had to copy. That line was the *hupogrammos*, the pattern which the boy must follow. Sometimes the writing was a moral maxim; more often it was a nonsense sentence which contained all the letters of the alphabet. Clement of Alexandria (*Stromateis* 5.8) gives an example of such a sentence: *marpte sphigx klōps zbuchthēdon*. (In Greek *ph, ps, ch* and *th* are all single letters, respectively *phi, psi, chi* and *theta*.) That was the perfect line of writing which the master wrote at the top of the page and which the schoolboy had to copy. So Peter is saying: 'Just as the schoolboy learns to write by copying the perfect copper-plate example, so we are scholars in the school of life, and we can only learn to live by copying the perfect pattern of life which Jesus gave to us.'

But there was another way of using the *hupogrammos* which has something to contribute to Peter's meaning. Quintilian in his *Education of an Orator* (1.1.27) tells us that sometimes the schoolmaster traced the letters in the wax of the tablet; and then the hand of the boy 'is guided along the grooves, for then he will make no mistakes'. At first the master helped the boy by placing his hand over the scholar's, but then he let him try it by himself and the edges of the grooves kept him from 'straying beyond the boundary'. That, too, must have been in Peter's mind. Simply to have to copy the *hupogrammos* all by oneself must often have been difficult and discouraging; but for the scholar to have had the master's hand over his hand, and to have had the grooves to follow, so that his pen could not stray, must have made things much easier. Jesus does not give us an example and leave it at that; an example can be the most discouraging thing on earth. For centuries men watched the birds flying and got no nearer to being able to do the same. A man may watch a champion golfer and be left with nothing but the desire to burn his own clubs! A pianist may hear and see a master executant and be left with nothing but the resolution never to touch a piano again! But Jesus does more than give us an example. As the master's hand guided the scholar's first fumbling efforts, so He guides us; as the groove kept the scholar's pen within the boundary, so His grace directs us. He left us not only a dauntingly perfect *hupogrammos*; He constantly helps us to follow it.

HUPOKRISIS AND HUPOKRITĒS

ACTING A PART

Hupokrisis and *hupokritēs* are the words which, in the NT, are translated 'hypocrisy' and 'hypocrite'. In the NT there is no sin more strongly condemned than hypocrisy, and in popular opinion there is no sin more universally detested.

The curious thing is that in classical Greek these words have no ill flavour and no bad meaning whatsoever; they are words which have definitely come down in the world; and yet we shall see that they had the seeds of their degradation in them. In classical Greek the basic meaning of *hupokritēs* is 'one who answers'. The verb *hupokrinesthai* is the standard word for 'to answer'. From that basic meaning *hupokritēs* develops the following regular meanings. (*a*) An interpreter or expounder of oracles or dreams. When Lucian tells his audience of the dream which made him into a writer, he says that they must be saying to themselves, 'Surely he does not take us for *oneirōn hupokritai*, interpreters, of dreams' (*Somnium*, 17). (*b*) An orator Demosthenes can be called by one of the critics an exceptional and many-talented *hupokritēs*. (*c*) A reciter or declaimer of poetry. In an age where there were no books the 'rhapsodists' recited the poems and the epics and they were *hupokritai*. (*d*) An actor. A play is a work which is made up of question and answer; and an actor can be described as a *hupokritēs*, an answerer. Now it is from this last meaning that *hupokritēs* develops its bad sense, and comes to mean a 'dissembler, one who is playing a part, putting on an act'.

In the Septuagint *hupokritēs* is definitely a bad word (Job 34.30; 36.13). By this time it has acquired a definitely unpleasant meaning; but it is essential to note that by the time the Septuagint was being revised *hupokritēs* has become, not only a bad word, but an *actively evil* word. One of the famous revisions of the Septuagint was made by a man called Aquila. In Job 15.34; Prov. 11.9; Isa. 33.14, Aquila has *hupokritēs* and the Septuagint has *asebēs*, which means nothing less than 'impious'. In Job 20.5 Aquila has *hupokritēs* and the Septuagint has *paranomos*, which means a 'transgressor', a 'law-breaker'. In Isa. 32.6 Aquila has *hupokrisis*, and the Septuagint has *anoma*, which means 'lawless things'. Clearly this word does not mean simply 'hypocrisy'; it has begun to stand for something evil, lawless, godless, actively malign. In the *Epistle of Barnabas* (2nd century A.D.) there is a description of 'The Two Ways' and in it it is said: 'You must not join yourself with those who walk in the way of death; you must hate everything that is not pleasing to God; you must hate all *hupokrisis*, and you must not abandon the commands of the Lord.' Obviously *hupokrisis* is active and evil sin.

In the NT *hupokrisis* and *hupokritēs* have certain definite lines of thought.

(i) The *hupokritēs* is the man who goes in for play-acting goodness, for what has been called 'theatrical goodness'. He is the man who wants everyone to see him give alms (Matt. 6.2), to see him pray (Matt. 6.5), to know that he is fasting (Matt. 6.16). He is the man whose goodness is designed, not to please God, but to please men, the man who says not 'To *God* be the glory' but, 'To *me* be the credit'.

(ii) The *hupokritēs* is the man who, in the very name of religion, breaks God's laws. He is the man who says that he cannot help his parents because he had dedicated his belongings to the service of God (Matt. 15.7; Mark 7.5). the man who refuses to help a sick person on the Sabbath, because it would be to break the Sabbath Law, although he will see to the comfort of his beasts on the Sabbath day (Luke 13.15). He is the man who prefers his idea of religion to God's idea.

(iii) The *hupokritēs* is the man who conceals his true motives under a cloak of pretence. The true motives of the people who asked Jesus the question about paying tribute were not to get information and guidance but to entangle Jesus in His words. They are *hupokritai* (Mark 12.15; Matt. 22.18). The *hupokritēs* is the subtle schemer with deceptive words.

(iv) The *hupokritēs* is the man who hides an evil heart under a cloak of piety. The Pharisees were like that (Matt. 23.28). He goes through the outward motions of religion while in his heart there is pride and arrogance, bitterness and hate. He is the kind of man who never fails to go to church and never fails to condemn a sinner. His is the pride that apes humility.

(v) The *hupokritēs* in the end becomes blind. He can read the weather signs but cannot read the signs of God (Luke 12.56). He has deceived others so often that in the end he has deceived himself.

(vi) The *hupokritēs* is the man, who in the cause of religion, seduces others from the right way (Gal. 2.13; I Tim. 4.2; I Pet. 2.1). He persuades others to listen to him instead of to God.

(vii) In the end the *hupokritēs* is the man who is under the condemnation of God (Matt. 24.51).

There is warning here. Of all sins 'hypocrisy' is the easiest to fall into, and of all sins it is most sternly condemned.

HUPOMONĒ

THE MANLY VIRTUE

Hupomonē is one of the noblest of NT words. Normally it is translated 'patience' or 'endurance', but, as we shall see, there is no single English word which transmits all the fullness of its meaning. In classical Greek it is not a very common word, it is used of the endurance of toil that has come upon a man all against his will, of endurance of the sting of grief, the shock of battle and the coming of death. It has one very interesting use—it is used of the ability of a plant to live under hard and unfavourable circumstances. In later Greek, in the later Jewish literature, it is specially common, for instance in Fourth Maccabees, of that quality of 'spiritual staying power' which enabled men to die for their God.

In the NT the noun *hupomonē* is used 30 times, and the corresponding verb *hupomenein* is used in this sense about 15 times. As we have said the normal translation of the noun is 'patience', and of the verb 'to endure', but when we examine its use in detail certain great truths, which are inspirations, begin to emerge.

(i) *Hupomonē* is very commonly used in connection with 'tribulation'. Tribulation worketh patience (Rom. 5.3). The Christian must approve himself in much 'patience' and in 'afflictions' (II Cor. 6.4). The Thessalonians are commended for their 'patience' and faith in 'persecutions' and 'tribulations' (II Thess. 1.4). The Christian must be patient (*hupomenein*) in 'tribulation'. This use is specially common in the Revelation, which is characteristically the martyr's book (cp. Rev. 1.9; 3.10; 13.10).

(ii) *Hupomonē* is used in connection with 'faith'. The testing of faith produces 'patience' (Jas. 1.3). It is *hupomonē* which perfects faith.

(iii) *Hupomonē* is used in connection with 'hope'. Tribulation begets 'patience' and patience begets experience and experience begets 'hope' (Rom. 5.3). It is 'patience' and comfort which produce 'hope' (Rom. 15.4, 5). The 'patience' of the 'hope' of the Thessalonians is praised (I Thess. 1.3).

(iv) *Hupomonē* is connected with 'joy'. The Christian life is marked with 'patience' and long-suffering with joyfulness (Col. 1.11).

(v) Oftenest of all *hupomonē* is connected with some goal of glory, some greatness which shall be. The references are too many to cite in full (Luke 21.19; Rom. 2.7; Heb. 10.36; 12.1; II Tim. 2.10, 12; Jas. 1.12; 5.11).

And now we can see the essence and the characteristic of this great virtue *hupomonē*. It is not the patience which can sit down and bow its head and let things descend upon it and passively endure until the storm is past. It is not, in the Scots word, merely 'tholing' things. It is the spirit which can bear things, not simply with resignation, but with blazing hope; it is not the spirit which sits statically enduring in the one place, but the spirit which bears things because it knows that these things are leading to a goal of glory; it is not the patience which grimly waits for the end, but the patience which radiantly hopes for the dawn. It has been called 'a masculine constancy under trial'. It has been said that always it has a background of *andreia,* which is courage. Chrysostom calls *hupomonē* a root of all the goods, mother of piety, fruit that never withers, a fortress that is never taken, a harbour that knows no storms'. He calls it 'the queen of virtues, the foundation of right actions, peace in war, calm in tempest, security in plots', and neither the violence of man nor the powers of the evil one can injure it. It is the quality which keeps a man on his feet with his face to the wind. It is the virtue which can transmute the hardest trial into glory because beyond the pain it sees the goal. George Matheson, who was stricken in blindness and disappointed in love, wrote a prayer in which he pleads that he might accept God's will, 'not with dumb resignation, but with holy joy; not only with the absence of murmur, but with a song of praise'. Only *hupomonē* can enable a man to do that.

KALEIN, KLĒTOS AND KLĒSIS

THE CALLING OF GOD

ONE of the most basic and fundamental of all NT conceptions is the conception of God's calling of men; and it is with that conception that these three words have to do. *Kalein* is the verb which means 'to call'; *klēsis* is the noun which means 'a call'; *klētos* is the adjective which means 'called'.

In classical Greek the verb *kalein* has four main usages, all of which have something to offer for our better understanding of the NT use of the term.

(i) *Kalein* is the regular verb for 'calling' a person or a place by a name. So in Matt. 1.21, 23, 25, Jesus is 'called' by the name 'Jesus'. In Matt. 5.9 the peacemakers are 'called' the sons or God. In Matt. 23.7 the scribes love to be 'called' Rabbi. This is the commonest of all the uses of *kalein*.

(ii) *Kalein* is the regular verb for 'summoning' or 'calling' a person. It may be that the person is 'summoned' to an office and an honour. Paul is 'called' to be an apostle (*klētos*) (Rom. 1.1; I Cor. 1.1). It may be that the person is 'summoned' to be given a task. In Matt. 25.14 the servants are 'called' to take over the estate when the master is away (cp. Luke 19.13). It may be that the person is summoned to be given a reward for his work and to give an account of it (Matt. 20.8). *Kalein* is regularly used for summoning a person to an office, a task, a responsibility, a reward, and an account.

(iii) *Kalein* is the regular verb for 'inviting a person to a meal or a banquet or into a house as a guest'. So much so is this the case that the past participle passive *ho keklēmenos* and the adjective *ho klētos* can both by themselves mean 'the guest' (for this use in the Septuagint cp. I Kings 1.41). So *kalein* is the word used for 'inviting' the guests to the wedding feast (Matt. 22.3). It is used of Simon the Pharisee 'inviting' Jesus to a meal in his house (Luke 7.39). It is the word that Luke uses of the humble and the conceited guests who are 'bidden' to a feast (Luke 14.8). It is the word that is used of those who are 'called' to the marriage supper of the Lamb (Rev. 19.9). *Kalein* is the regular word which is used for a hospitable invitation.

(iv) *Kalein* is the regular word for 'summoning into the law-courts'. It is the word that is used for 'citing' a witness or a defendant to appear before a judge. In the NT it is so used of Peter and John being brought before the Sanhedrin (Acts 4.18); and of Paul being summoned before Felix to face his Jewish prosecutors (Acts 24.2). It is the word which is used when a man is summoned to stand his trial and to give account.

Even if we were to stop here and go no further we would have a flood of light on what the call of the Christian means. We could say four things at least.

(i) The Christian is a man who hears the summons of God. Now the very essence of a summons is that it is either a challenge or an appeal. A man can either accept it or reject it; he can heed it or disregard it; he can listen to it or be deaf to it. The very word lays upon us the tremendous responsibility of answering—or not answering—the voice of God.

(ii) The Christian life is a summons to duty. Always the Christian is summoned to a task. God is always offering the Christian man a task to do. In Cicero's *Republic* (1.20, 23) Laelius is asked: 'What then do you think we ought to teach the people we have to educate?' And the answer is: 'We ought to teach these arts which will make us of use to the state.' The call of God is a call to the Christian to be of use in this world.

(iii) The call of God is a call to privilege. *Kalein* and *klēsis* are intimately associated with the invitation to a feast, a banquet, the welcome to a table and a home. The call of God to the Christian is the call to come and to enjoy His fellowship, His hospitality, the joy and the fullness of being a guest of God.

(iv) The call of God is a call to judgment. Equally *kalein* and *klēsis* are intimately associated with being cited to appear before a judge and a court. The Christian life is not going nowhere; it is going to the judgment seat of God. And if a man disregards the call of God, if he is deaf to the summons to duty, if he is heedless to the invitation of God, there comes the final call, the call which will call him to account.

The supreme interest and illumination of these words is the connections in which they are used.

(i) The 'call' which comes to the Christian is the call of God and God alone. It does not come to him because he deserved it, but simply because God knew him and called him. Jacob is not chosen because of any superior achievement to Esau, but simply because God called him (Rom. 9.11). Our own calling goes back directly to the will of God (Rom. 8.30).

(ii) Another way to put it is that the call of God is associated with *charis*, with 'grace' (Gal. 1.6; 1.15). It is not as if God chose us because we stood out because of special goodness or special attainment. It is out of the goodness of His heart that God calls us who never deserved to be called. God's invitation is an invitation to which we have no claim at all. Not our merit, but God's love, is the moving force of this call.

(iii) The 'call' is associated with *eirēnē*, with 'peace'

(I Cor. 7.15; Col. 3.15). Now in the NT sense 'peace' is not just the absence of trouble; it is everything that makes for our highest good. It was said of Robert Burns that he was *haunted* and not *helped* by his religion. God's call is to help us to be what we ought to be to Him and to our fellow men.

(iv) The 'call' is associated with *koinōnia*, with 'fellowship' (I Cor. 1.9). That fellowship is a double fellowship; it is a fellowship with Christ and with our fellow men. The man who hears and answers the call of God is on the way to being in a new relationship with Christ and with his fellow men.

(v) The 'call' is associated with *eleutheria*, with 'freedom' (Gal. 5.13). To answer God's call is to find, not slavery, but liberation. The man who responds to the invitation of God is freed from self, and sin and Satan.

(vi) The 'call' is associated with *elpis*, with 'hope' (Eph. 4.4). When a man hears and answers the call of God it is the end of pessimism and the end of despair. He is no longer an inevitably defeated man; he is a potentially victorious man. He no longer lives a life encircled by endless frustrations; he lives a life enlarged with endless possibilities.

(vii) The 'call' is associated with 'duty'. Again and again we are urged to walk in a way that is worthy of our calling (Eph. 4.1; I Cor. 7.17). It is a call to follow in the footsteps of Jesus Christ (I Pet. 2.21). It is a call, not to *akatharsia*, which is 'uncleanness', but to *hagiasmos*, which is 'sanctification' (I Thess. 4.7). The man who hears and answers this call sets out on the road to holiness. The one who calls us is *hagios*, 'holy', and we who are called must also be *hagios*, 'holy' (I Pet. 1.15). We must be counted 'worthy of this calling' (II Thess. 1.11). For that very reason it is something which, by our lives, we must for ever strive to make secure (II Pet. 1.10). Think of it this way. A man might receive a gift which he well knew he did not deserve; he might be given something of such a munificent generosity that he knew that he could never repay it; he might be treated with a kindness that he knew that he had not even remotely earned. For that very reason he will be bound to spend all his strength and all his life in one passionate effort to show how grateful he is for the gift that he never deserved. His effort is not the result of fear; it is not the the product of the desire for credit; it is simply the inevitable result of an amazed and wondering love. So then we well know that nothing that we have done or can do can make us deserve to be called by God. That is all the more reason why all life should be spent in the effort to be worthy of the love which so honoured us against all our deserving.

There are certain further things that we must still note about this idea of 'the calling of God'.

(i) The 'call' is associated with salvation (*sōzein*) (II Tim. 1.9). To hear and answer the call is at one and the same time to be saved from the penalty of sin and armed with strength for life for the future. It is a call which rescues from penalty and which clothes with power. Now 'salvation' is something which is eschatological. That is to say, it begins on this earth, but it goes beyond this earth. It has its beginning in time, but it has its consummation in eternity; and there are a number of associations of this group of words with conceptions and ideas which embrace both this world and the next.

(ii) The Christians are people who are 'called to be saints' (*klētoi hagioi*). Now *hagios* literally means 'separated'; a person who is *hagios* in the Christian sense of the term is a person who has separated himself from the world in order to consecrate himself to God. Sainthood, in the NT sense of the term, is concerned, not so much with where a man is, but with the direction in which he is facing. The Christian is called to be a man the direction of whose life is towards God, who lives with God now, and who will see God face to face hereafter.

(iii) The Christian is called 'out of darkness into light' (I Pet. 2.9). He is called out of the shadows of the world's sin and frustration and death into the light of the knowledge and the life of God. The Christian is the man who is living, not in the twilight of the gathering dark, but in the light of the breaking dawn.

(iv) The Christian is called 'to eternal life and to an

eternal inheritance' (I Tim. 6.12; Heb. 9.15). In the NT the word 'eternal' (*aiōnios*) has much more to with *quality* than *duration* of life. We may put it this way. *Aiōnios*, 'eternal', is the word which properly and uniquely belongs to God; therefore 'eternal life' is the kind of life which belongs to God. The Christian is 'called' out of this troubled, soiled, frustrated, dying life into the blessedness of the life of God Himself.

(v) Sometimes this is put in other ways. The Christian is 'called' by God to 'honour' (Heb. 9.15). He is 'called' to obtain 'the glory of our Lord Jesus Christ' (II Thess. 2.14). He is 'called' to obtain 'the eternal glory of God' (I Pet. 5.10). The Christian is a man who is called to glory. The calling of God makes great demands, but equally it makes tremendous promises. 'Glory' is everything that heaven offers. The Christian is invited to share nothing less than the splendour of the life of God. The NT thinks not so much of the punishment that a man will suffer if he refuses the call, but far more of the splendour he will miss.

(vi) Sometimes this call will come to men through men. Paul tells the Thessalonians that 'their call' came through 'his gospel' (II Thess. 2.14). It is the great glory of the Christian that he can, if he will, transmit to others the call that he has himself heard. The Christian—and that does not mean only the preacher—can be the bearer of God's invitation to glory to his fellow-men.

We may finally note that twice this word *kalein* is used of Jesus.

(i) It is used of 'the call of the disciples' (Matt. 4.21). (ii) It is used of 'the call to repentance' (Luke 5.32). Jesus calls men to fellowship with Himself and to a life which is a new life. The Christian is called to be Christ's friend and is therefore called to be a new man. The two things go together. The Christian life is at one and the same time an invitation to privilege, to responsibility and to glory. And at the back of it there remains the haunting thought that the tragedy of life is to refuse the invitation of God.

KATARTIZEIN

THE WORD OF CHRISTIAN DISCIPLINE

THE great practical interest of *katartizein* lies in the fact that it is the word used in Gal. 6.1, for, as the AV puts it, 'restoring' a brother who is taken in fault. If, then, we can penetrate into its meaning it will greatly assist us in forming a correct view of the method and purpose of Christian discipline.

In classical Greek it has a wide variety of meanings, all of which can be gathered together under one or other of two heads. (i) It means 'to adjust, to put in order, to restore'. Hence it is used of pacifying a city which is torn by faction; of setting a limb that has been dislocated; of developing certain parts of the body by exercise; of restoring a person to his rightful mind; of reconciling friends who have become estranged. (ii) It is used of 'equipping or fully furnishing someone or something for some given purpose.' So it is used of fitting out a ship and it is used of an army, fully armed and equipped, and drawn up in battle-array. Its uses in the papyri do not add greatly to our insight into its meaning. There, too, it is used of something 'prepared for a given purpose or person'. It is, for instance, so used of clothes which have been made and prepared for someone to wear.

In the NT it is used about thirteen times, twice in quotations from the OT (Matt. 21.16; Heb. 10.5). It has three main lines of usage.

(i) It is the word which is used of the disciples 'mending their nets' (Matt. 4.21; Mark 1.19). It may possibly there mean that they were 'folding up the nets'. But whether it means mending or folding up the idea is that the nets were being prepared for future use.

(ii) There is a set of passages in which the basic meaning is that of equipment. In Luke 6.40 it is said that a scholar cannot turn out better equipped than his teacher. Rom. 9.22 speaks of vessels of wrath equipped for destruction.

(iii) There is a set of passages in which the AV translates it 'to perfect' (II Cor. 13.11; I Thess. 3.10; Heb. 13.21; I Pet. 5.10).

(iv) There is one passage in I Cor. 1.10 where the AV translates it 'perfectly joined together'. It is there used of the drawing together of the discordant elements in the Corinthian Church; and the idea could be either that of setting together dislocated and broken limbs, or that of calming and pacifying the warring elements in a disturbed city.

Now when we take this and apply it to Christian discipline certain most significant things emerge. (i) It is clear that Christian discipline is never meant to be merely retributory punishment; it is not simply vengeance on the evil-doer. (ii) Discipline is meant to 'mend' a man and to 'repair' him. It regards him more as something which has been damaged or injured than it does as a deliberate sinner. (iii) Discipline is meant to 'equip' him better to meet his temptations and to meet the battle and the demands of life. It regards him as a man ill and inadequately equipped and it regards the duty of the Christian society as being that of sending him out better able to deal with the things which defeated him. (iv) It regards the evil-doer as one imperfectly constructed to deal with life and it calls on the Christian community to give him a more perfect knowledge and more perfect strength to overcome evil and to do the right.

So, then, when we study this word, we see that Christian discipline is never vengeful and retributory and sadistic. It is always constructive. It is applied always and only for the sake of helping the man who has erred to do better.

KATHAROS

THE LIFE THAT IS CLEAN

Katharos, which means 'pure' or 'clean', is one of the great Greek words. It occurs about 24 times in the NT;

but before ever it became a Christian word it had a rich variety of meanings, all of which contribute something to its meaning for us.

(i) Let us look at *katharos* in classical Greek. (*a*) It began in Homer by meaning simply 'physically clean', as a man's body or clothes are clean. (*b*) It goes on to mean 'pure', in the sense of free from any admixture. Often it is used of clear water; sometimes it is used of the sunlight and of the clean wind; it is the word for 'white' bread; it is regularly used of grain that has been winnowed, of metals that are without alloy and of feelings that are unmixed. Every one of these meanings contributes something to the full Christian meaning of the word. (*c*) It is used in the sense of 'free from debt'. A man who has paid all his accounts and taxes and on whom no man has a claim is *katharos*. To make someone *katharos* is to give him a discharge from a debt or to acquit him of a charge. (*d*) It means 'free from all guilt and pollution'. It is used of innocent hands, of a body and a soul that are morally clean. (*e*) It means 'ceremonially clean', that is to say fit to approach God, or fit for the worship of God. So it is used of the altar, of the sacrifice, of the worshipper who has carried out the correct ritual, of the days on which sacrifice might be offered. It describes something which is fit for the service of God. (*f*) It means 'pure in blood' or 'genuine'. It is used of someone whose race is pure; it is used of a saying whose authenticity cannot be doubted.

(ii) Let us look at *katharos* in the papyri. (*a*) It is used of all kinds of things in the sense of 'clean', 'pure', 'without blemish'. A man writes, 'I have examined the goat and I certify it with my seal as *katharos*, unblemished, physically perfect.' A man promises, 'I will give you back the fields as *katharos*, clean, as I got them.' (*b*) It is used of a document that is corrected and 'free of errors'. It would be the word for a corrected proof. (*c*) It is used of 'the conditions of entry to a temple'. 'First, and greatest of all, the worshippers must have their hands and their minds pure and sound, and must have no terrible thing upon their consciences.'

(iii) Now let us look at it in the NT. (*a*) It is used of

physical cleanness. The linen sheet in which they laid Jesus' body was *katharos* (Matt. 27.59, cp. Matt. 23.26; Rev. 19.8). (*b*) It is used in the sense of 'clean' with the meaning, when used of persons, that they are fit for God's service and worship, and when used of things, that they are fit for the Christians to use (John 13.10; Luke 11.41; Rom. 14.20; Tit. 1.15). (*c*) It is used in the sense of 'innocent of any crime' (Acts 18.6; 20.26). (*d*) It is used of 'the heart and the conscience' being pure and clean (I Tim. 1.5; 3.9; II Tim. 1.3; 2.22; I Pet. 1.22). (*e*) It is used of a worship which is fit to be offered to God (Jas. 1.27).

But the instance in the NT which means most to us is its use in the Beatitude, 'Blessed are the *katharoi* (plural) in heart, for they shall see God' (Matt. 5.8). How are we to explain this, and what meaning are we to give *katharos* here? A word is always known by the company it keeps. There are four Greek words with which *katharos* is often closely associated. (*a*) There is *alēthinos*, which means 'real', 'genuine', as opposed to that which is unreal and, as we would say, a fake. (*b*) There is *amigēs*, which means 'pure', 'unmixed'. This word is used, for instance, of pure, unalloyed pleasure. And it is used of a roll which has in it the work of only one author. (*c*) It is used with *akratos*. This is the word that describes pure wine or pure milk which has not been adulterated by water. It is pure in the sense of 'neat', completely unadulterated. (*d*) It is used with *akēratos*, which is the word that describes unalloyed gold, hair which has never been shorn, an unmown meadow, a virgin whose chastity has never been doubted.

Now all these words basically describe something which is pure from every taint and admixture of evil. How then shall we translate, Blessed are the *katharoi* in heart? We must think of it this way—Blessed are those whose motives are absolutely unmixed, whose minds are utterly sincere, who are completely and totally single-minded. What a summons to self-examination is here! Here is the most demanding Beatitude of all. When we examine our motives with honesty, it will humiliate us, for an unmixed motive is the rarest thing in the world. But the blessedness is to the man with the motive that is as pure as clean water, and with the single-mindedness which does everything as to God. That is the standard by which this word and this Beatitude demand that we should measure ourselves.

KOINŌNIA, KOINŌNEIN AND KOINŌNOS

THE CHRISTIAN FELLOWSHIP

IN the NT there is a great group of words all of which have to do with the basic idea of 'fellowship'. There is the word *koinōnia*. In classical Greek *koinōnia* means an association or a partnership. Plato uses the phrase the *koinōnia* of women with men for 'co-education'. Human *koinōnia* is the Greek for human society. The word is also used to express the idea of community. Plato says, 'There must be a certain *koinōnia* between pleasure and pain.' In later Greek *koinōnia* is used as the opposite and contrast to *pleonexia*, which is the grasping spirit which is out for itself. *Koinōnia* is the spirit of generous sharing as contrasted with the spirit of selfish getting. In the contemporary colloquial Greek *koinōnia* has three distinctive meanings. (i) It means very commonly a 'business partnership'. In a papyrus announcement a man speaks of his brother 'with whom I have no *koinōnia*', no business connection. (ii) It is used specially of 'marriage'. Two people enter into marriage in order to have '*koinōnia* of life', that is to say, to live together a life in which everything is shared. (iii) It is used of a man's 'relationship with God'. Epictetus talks of religion as 'aiming to have *koinōnia* with Zeus'. So in secular Greek *koinōnia* is used to express a close and intimate relationship into which people enter. In the NT *koinōnia* occurs some eighteen times. When we examine the connections in which it is used we come to see how wide and far-stretching is the fellowship which should characterize the Christian life.

(i) In the Christian life there is a *koinōnia* which means 'a sharing of friendship' and an abiding in the company of others (Acts 2.42; II Cor. 6.14). It is very interesting to note that that friendship is based on common Christian knowledge (I John 1.3). Only those who are friends with Christ can really be friends with each other.

(ii) In the Christian life there is a *koinōnia* which means 'practical sharing' with those less fortunate. Paul three times uses the word in connection with the collection he took from his churches for the poor saints at Jerusalem (Rom. 15.26; II Cor. 8.4; II Cor. 9.13; cp. Heb. 13.16). The Christian fellowship is a *practical* thing.

(iii) In the Christian life there is a *koinōnia* which is a 'partnership in the work of Christ' (Phil. 1.5). Paul gives thanks for the partnership of the Philippians in the work of the gospel.

(iv) In the Christian life there is a *koinōnia* 'in the faith'. The Christian is never an isolated unit; he is one of a believing company (Eph. 3.9).

(v) In the Christian life there is a 'fellowship (*koinōnia*) in the Spirit' (II Cor. 13.14; Phil. 2.1). The Christian lives in the presence, the company, the help and the guidance of the Spirit.

(vi) In the Christian life there is a *koinōnia* 'with Christ'. Christians are called to the *koinōnia* of Jesus Christ, the Son of God (I Cor. 1.9). That fellowship is found specially through the Sacrament (I Cor. 10.16). The cup and the bread are supremely the *koinōnia* of the body and the blood of Christ. In the sacrament above all Christians find Christ and find each other. Further, that fellowship with Christ is fellowship with His sufferings (Phil. 3.10). When the Christian suffers he has, amidst the pain, the joy of knowing that he is sharing things with Christ.

(vii) In the Christian life there is *koinōnia* 'with God' (I John 1.3). But it is to be noted that that fellowship is ethically conditioned, for it is not for those who have chosen to walk in darkness (I John 1.6).

The Christian *koinōnia* is that bond which binds Christians to each other, to Christ and to God.

There are other two great NT words in the *koinōnia* group at which we must look. The first is the verb *koinōnein*. In classical Greek *koinōnein* means 'to have a share in a thing'. It is used, for instance, of two people who have all things in common; it is used of 'going shares' with someone, and therefore of having 'business dealings' with him. It is used of 'sharing an opinion' with someone, and therefore agreeing with him. In the contemporary Greek of the papyri it has three main meanings. (i) It means to share 'in an action' with someone. For instance, when the authorities cannot trace down some malefactors they come to the conclusion that those who 'share' in their misdeeds are sheltering them. (ii) It is user of sharing in 'a common possession'. For instance, all men are said to 'share' in human nature. (iii) It is used of the sharing of 'life'. A doctor puts up a tablet to a wife who had practised with him, for, he writes, 'I *shared* all life with you alone.'

When we turn to the NT, we once again see how wide this Christian sharing is. (i) All men share in 'human nature' (Heb. 2.14). There is a community between men simply in virtue of the fact that they are men. (ii) The Christians share in 'material things' (Rom. 12.13, 15.27; Gal. 6.6). It is interesting to note that of its eight appearances in the NT, four deal with this practical teaching. No Christian can bear to have too much while others have too little. (iii) It is used of sharing in 'an action' (I Tim. 5.22). We are partners with each other and with God. (iv) It is used of sharing 'an experience' (I Pet. 4.13). The man who suffers for his faith, in that very suffering shares the experience of Jesus Christ.

Koinōnos in classical Greek means a companion, a partner or a joint-owner. In the papyri it has come to be most commonly used of a business partner. For instance, a certain Hermes takes Cornelius as his *koinōnos* in a fishing lake to the extent of one-sixth of a share. A father complains to his son in regard to their allotment that their *koinōnos* is not doing his share of the work. It is to be remembered that in contemporary secular Greek the word is almost entirely a *business* word.

In the NT it occurs ten times. (i) It is used in the sense of a sharer 'in an action or course of action'. Jesus says that the Pharisees claim that if they had lived in the days when their fathers killed the prophets they would not have 'shared' in such an action (Matt. 23.30; cp I Cor. 10.18, 10.20. (ii) It is used in the sense of 'a partner'. James and John are Peter's *koinōnoi* in the fishing business (Luke 5.10). Paul describes Titus as his *koinōnos* and *sunergos,* his *partner* and his fellow-worker (II Cor. 8.23). Paul's claim on Philemon, when he is pleading for Onesimus, is that Philemon is his *koinōnos* (Phil. 17). The Christian looks on all fellow-Christians as partners in a great work. For him to call a fellow man 'partner' is the most natural thing in the world. (iii) It is used in the sense of a sharer in 'an experience' (II Cor. 1.7; Heb. 10.33). Nothing happens to us alone. It happens to all men and it happened to Jesus Christ. Between Christ and man and man and man there is that sympathy of those who have passed through a common experience. (iv) Once it is used of man's sharing in the divine nature (II Pet. 1.4). Men share not only in the things of earth but in the glory of heaven.

Surely there is no more gracious group of words than this. The Christian shares in the manhood of all men; he shares in the common experience of joy and tears; he shares in the things divine and in the glory that shall be; and all his life he must be a sharer of all he has, for he knows that his true wealth lies in what he gives away.

LEITOURGIA

THE CHRISTIAN SERVICE

Leitourgia, from which comes our English word 'liturgy', and its kindred words form a group of words of unsurpassed interest. In classical and hellenistic Greek these words go through four stages of meaning. (i) In the very early days *leitourgein,* the verb, meant to undertake some service of the state voluntarily and of one's own free will, voluntarily to shoulder some public task in order patriotically to serve the state. (ii) Later *leitourgein* came to mean to perform the services which the State laid upon citizens specially qualified to perform them. The services were the same, but now instead of being voluntary they have become compulsory. Certain duties were liable to be laid on any citizen who possessed more than three talents, that is about £700.

Four typical such duties were: (*a*) *Chorēgia*, which meant the supplying of all the expenses to maintain and train a chorus for the great dramatic performances. (*b*) *Gymnasarchia*, which meant the paying of the expenses involved in the training of outstanding athletes for the games. (*c*) *Architheōria*, which was the defraying of the expenses of embassies sent out by the state on solemn or sacred occasions. (*d*) *Triērarchia*, which meant the shouldering of all the expenses of a trireme or warship in time of national crisis. Still later, especially in Egypt, nearly all municipal duties were *leitourgiai*. The state picked out a suitable man and laid on him the duty of serving in some capacity his town or village or county. (iii) Still later *leitourgein* came to describe any kind of service. It is used, for instance, of dancing girls, flute-players, musicians who are hired for some entertainment; of a workman working for any master; and even, strangely enough, of a prostitute giving her services. (iv) In NT times *leitourgein* was the regular word for the service that a priest or servant rendered in a temple of the gods. So we read of 'Thaues and Taous, the twins, who *serve* in the great temple of Serapis at Memphis'.

In the NT the words have three main uses. (i) They are used of the service rendered by man to man. So Paul, when he is set on taking the collection for the poor saints of Jerusalem, uses *leitourgein* and *leitourgia* (Rom. 15.27; II Cor. 9.12). He uses them of the service of the Philippians and of Epaphroditus to himself (Phil. 2.17, 30). To serve others is a 'liturgy' laid on the citizen of the Kingdom by God. (ii) They are used of specifically religious service (Luke 1.23; Acts 13.2). They are actually used of the high-priestly work of Jesus Himself (Heb. 8.6; 8.2). Our Church work is a 'liturgy' again laid on us by God. (iii) There are two specially interesting uses in Paul. (*a*) The magistrate, the person in power, is called by Paul a *leitourgos* (Rom. 13.6) A man's public service must be done for God. (*b*) Paul uses it of himself when he calls himself Jesus Christ's *leitourgos* to the Gentiles (Rom. 15.16). Just as Athens in the old days sent out its *leitourgoi* to represent the state, so Paul is sent by God to the Gentiles. Perhaps the most interesting fact of all about the word *leitourgos* is that in later Greek it came simply to mean a 'workman', for that simple fact has in it the great truth that all work is a 'liturgy' laid on men by God, and that the commonest task is glorious because it is done for Him.

The great fact about *leitourgia* is that it has a double background. (i) It describes voluntary service, spontaneously shouldered. (ii) It describes that service which the state lays compulsorily upon its citizens. The Christian is a man who works for God and men, first, because he desires to, with his whole heart, and second, because he is compelled to, because the love of Christ constrains him.

LUTRON, LUTROUN AND APOLUTRŌSIS

THE DEBT AND ITS PAYMENT

THERE is a group of NT words which all have to do with the idea of ransom and redemption, of deliverance and freedom won and purchased at a price. These words have been so influential in moulding the conception of the work of Jesus Christ, and of the idea of the atonement, that it is absolutely necessary to study them in detail. We begin with the word *lutron*.

(i) In classical Greek the word occurs mostly in the plural (*lutra*) and its basic meaning is 'the price of release'. The title of the 24th book of the *Iliad* is *Lutra Hektoros*, 'the ransoming of Hector', and it tells the story of the ransoming of the dead body of Hector, the Trojan champion, after it had been captured by the Greeks. So in classical Greek there are a whole series of phrases—*labein lutra tinos*, to receive a ransom for someone, *lutra didonai tinos*, to give a ransom for someone, *aneu lutrōn aphienai*, to let go without a ransom, and the phrase *huper lutrōn* describes a sum paid 'as a ransom'. Nearly always in classical Greek the word is quite literal; it means the price paid to effect someone's deliverance. The late Greek lexicon *Suidas* defines *lutron* quite simply as *misthos*, which means 'pay' or 'price', and goes on to amplify it by saying that it means 'Those things which are offered for freedom in order to ransom a man from barbarian slavery'. Very rarely in classical Greek it has a semi-metaphorical sense. Once it occurs in Aeschylus, the tragic poet, 'What *lutron* can there be for blood which has fallen upon the ground?' (*Choephoroi* 48). There it means, What release can there be for the guilty from the wrath and the defilement which follow upon shed blood?

(ii) Now to any NT writer this word would have two backgrounds. It would have a background from OT thought and usage. In the Septuagint the word occurs about eighteen times. If a man was the owner of an ox which was known to be dangerous and the ox gored and killed someone, because it had not been properly confined, the man's own life was forfeit unless he paid a *lutron*, 'blood money', to ransom himself (Ex. 21.30). If a man deliberately murdered another there could be no *lutron* for him, he must be executed (Num. 35.31, 32). If an Israelite in his poverty sold himself to a wealthy sojourner a wealthier relative could buy him out, and the price was a *lutron* (Lev. 25.51). A jealous man set on vengeance will accept no *lutron* in place of revenge (Prov. 6.35). *Lutron* is the ransom of captives taken in war (Isa. 45.13). But in the OT the word has one specially interesting use. According to the Jewish law the first-born of man and every creature was sacred to God. Num. 3.13 traces this back to God's sparing of the first-born sons of the Jews on the night of the first Passover in Egypt. If all the first-born sons were dedicated to the special service of God it would disrupt life altogether and so there was a ceremony called 'The Redemption of the First-born', by which the parents could buy back their son by a payment of five shekels to the priests (Num. 18.16).

Now that payment is regularly called a *lutron* (Num. 3.12, 46, 48, 49, 51; 18.15).

It may be laid down, as a general rule, that in the Greek OT the word *lutron* never has anything other than a literal meaning. It always means a payment which releases a man from an obligation which otherwise he was bound to fulfil. In the OT the *lutron* may be paid by the man himself, or it may be paid by someone for him; but always it is a price and a payment which releases him from a debt and a liability which otherwise he would have been bound to satisfy.

We now turn to the background which *lutron* had in Greek thought and practice. In the contemporary Greek of the NT times it has two main uses. (*a*) It is regularly used of 'the price which is paid to redeem something which is in pledge or in pawn' (*b*) It is regularly used of 'the purchase price paid or received for the liberation of a slave'. So a papyrus reads, 'I have given Helene her liberty and I have received *huper lutrōn autēs,* as the purchase price for her,' and then follows the actual sum of money received.

Now here we have to take account of another Greek custom in NT times which gives to NT language one of its most vivid pictures. There are another two NT words that we must bring in here—*agorazein* or *exagorazein,* which means 'to buy', and *timē,* which means 'price'. In I Cor. 6.19, 20, Paul says, 'Know ye not . . . that ye are not your own? For ye are bought (*agorazein*) with a price (*timē*)?' In I Cor. 7.23 he writes, 'Ye are bought (*agorazein*) with a price (*timē*); be not ye the servants of men?' In Gal. 3.13 he says that 'Christ has redeemed (*exagorazein*) us from the curse of the law'. In Gal. 4.4, 5 he says that God sent His Son 'to *redeem* them that were under the law'. In Gal. 5.1 he says, as it should be translated, 'For freedom (*ep'eleutheria*) did Christ set us free.' And in Gal. 5.13 he says, 'Ye were called for freedom (*ep'eleutheria*).' There are a great many Greek inscriptions which speak about a person being sold to a God, e.g. to Athene, to Asclepius, to Apollo. There was one special way in which a Greek slave could obtain his freedom. He could scrape and save, perhaps for years, such little sums as he was able to earn; and, as he saved the money, he deposited it little by little in the temple of some god. When he had laboriously amassed his complete purchase price, he took his master to the temple where the money was deposited. There the priest paid over to the master the purchase price of freedom, and the man who had been a slave became the property of the god and therefore 'free of all men'. There is an inscription on the wall of the temple of Apollo at Delphi like this: 'Apollo the Pythian, *bought* from Sosibus of Amphissa, for freedom (*ep'eleutheria*) a female slave, whose name is Nicaea, with a price (*timē*) of three minae of silver and a half-mina. Former seller according to the law: Eumnastus of Amphissa. The price (*timē*) he hath received. The purchase, however, Nicaea has committed to Apollo, for freedom (*ep'eleutheria*).' The purchase price was paid and Nicaea was the property of Apollo and free of all men. It is precisely this to which Paul indirectly refers when repeatedly he calls himself and others *doulos Christou*, 'the slave of Christ'. He has been bought by Christ and has become His property. It is very significant how Paul uses the very phrase *ep'eleutheria*, 'for freedom', which occurs again and again in these inscriptions. The purchase price is paid and the Christian belongs to Christ and is therefore free from all the powers which held him.

(iii) Now in the NT itself this word *lutron* occurs twice. In Mark 10.45 and Matt. 20.28 Jesus says that He came to give His life a *lutron*, 'a ransom', for many. There is one other kindred word which is used, the word *antilutron*. In I Tim. 2.6 we read of Christ Jesus who gave Himself an *antilutron*, 'a ransom', for all. *Antilutron* is a very rare word. It is worth noting in the passing that in the Orphic literature it is used to mean an 'antidote' and 'remedy'. Christ's death, we could understand it, is the 'antidote' for the poison, and the 'remedy' for the disease of sin.

There are still other words which we must carefully examine. But, even at this stage, we can lay this down—that Jesus Christ by His life and by His death released man from an obligation, a liability and a debt which otherwise he would have been bound to pay, and delivered him from a bondage and a slavery, by paying the purchase price of freedom which he himself could never have paid.

We must now consider the verb *lutroun.*

(i) In Greek, verbs have three voices and not, as in English, only two. In Greek a verb can be active or passive, as in English, but it can also be middle. Generally speaking, the middle voice has a kind of semi-reflexive sense; it means to do something for oneself, for one's own interest, or pleasure or profit. So in classical Greek the word *lutroun* has really three meanings. (i) In the active *lutroun* means to 'hold to ransom'. (ii) In the passive it means 'to be ransomed'. (iii) In the middle it means 'to ransom for oneself', that is 'to redeem' or 'rescue' by paying the necessary price. It is to be noted that the whole background of the word is 'captivity'. It has always got to do with rescuing, redeeming, liberating, ransoming a man or a thing from some hostile power which has him or it in its possession.

(ii) In the papyri the characteristic use of *lutroun* is 'to redeem a pledge'. It can be used of redeeming a person's clothes or cloak or property which have been deposited in pawn or pledge with someone. Again the word has this idea of getting something back into the possession of its rightful owner, rescuing something from the power and possession of an alien possessor.

(iii) In the Septuagint the word is very common, occurring more than 65 times. It has certain characteristic usages. (*a*) It is constantly used of 'God's redeeming of Israel from slavery in Egypt'. In Ex. 6.6 it is God's promise, 'I will redeem you with a stretched-out arm.' Over and over again the people are reminded that God 'redeemed' them 'out of the house of bondmen' (Deut. 7.8; 13.5). It is God's command that they must never forget that they were bondmen in the land of Egypt and that He 'redeemed' them (Deut. 15.15; 24.18). (*b*) It is constantly used of 'redeeming', 'buying back the first-born from the special service of God' (Ex. 13.13; 34.20). (*c*) It is constantly used of 'redeeming something that has been pledged and pawned' (Lev. 25.25, 30, 33). (*d*) In Israel a man could 'devote' something to God. He could devote an animal, a house, his money, even himself to the exclusive possession of God. That is what Jephthah did when he sacrificed his daughter to God (Judg. 12.29-40). Now it might be that after a man had devoted something to God he might want that thing back for his own use. He could get it back by making certain payments to the priests; and *lutroun* is used for buying back the thing that has been devoted to God (Lev. 27.15-33). (*e*) It is to be noted that once again *lutroun* so far, always describes the process of getting back something which has passed into the power and possession of someone else. But in the Septuagint the word has one very special use which is not literal at all. Over and over again *lutroun* is the word which is used in the Psalms and in the Prophets for God's deliverance and preservation of his people in the time of their trouble and distress. It is the Psalmist's prayer, '*Redeem* Israel, O God, out of all his troubles' (Ps. 25.22; cp. 26.11; 69.18; 130.8). It is the Psalmist's great thanksgiving that God has so redeemed him. 'Thou hast redeemed me, O Lord God of truth' (Ps. 31.5). It is God who *redeems* his life from destruction (Ps. 103.4; 55.18). This usage goes on into the prophets (Isa. 43.1; 44.22; Jer. 15.21; 50.34). So much so is this the case that *ho lutroumenos* (the present participle of the verb), 'the redeeming one', becomes almost a technical name for God. We will see more clearly and vividly what this means if we translate it, not 'redeem' but 'rescue'. God is the redeemer who rescues man from the troubles which have him in their grip.

(iv) In the NT the word occurs three times. In Luke 24.21 the grief-stricken wayfarers tell the unrecognized Jesus that they had hoped that Jesus would have been the one who would 'redeem' Israel. In Tit. 2.14 Jesus died that He might rescue us from all lawlessness. In I Pet. 1.18 the Christians are said to have been 'rescued' from their vain way of life.

We have still one other great NT word to examine. But once again we have arrived at the same conclusion. The word *lutroun* expresses the 'redeeming', 'rescuing' of a man from a power or a situation which has him in its grip and from which he is powerless to free himself.

Apolutrōsis is one of the great NT words. It literally means a 'ransoming' or a 'redeeming', but this time we are dealing with a word which has practically no history. It is only used in very late Greek, and that very rarely. When it is used it is used of the ransoming of captives taken in battle. In the papyri no instances at all are quoted. In the Septuagint it occurs only once—in Dan. 4.30 where it is used of the recovery of Nebuchadnezzar from illness. But in the NT it is used ten times and all its usages are significant. We will look at the most significant of them.

(i) It is used of our 'redemption from sin', and always in connection with the work of Jesus Christ. In Eph. 1.7 Paul says that the Christian has 'redemption' through the blood of Jesus Christ, 'the forgiveness of sins'. Exactly the same phrase is used in Col. 1.14. The same idea occurs in Heb. 9.15. The forgiveness of sins is indissolubly connected with the death of Christ.

(ii) It is used of 'the new relationship of friendship' into which man enters with God through the work of Jesus Christ. Paul speaks of the Christian entering into the right relationship with God, freely, by His grace, through the 'redemption' which is in Jesus Christ (Rom. 3.24).

(iii) It implies, not only forgiveness for past sins, but 'new, changed life for the future'. It implies adoption into the family of God (Rom. 8.23). For us Christ is made wisdom and justification and consecration and 'redemption' (I Cor. 1.30). *Apolutrōsis* looks, not only backwards to forgiveness, but forwards to a re-created life.

(iv) *Apolutrōsis* does not end with this life. It is eschatological. It is the foretaste of a process and a glory which will find their consummation in the coming of Christ and in the heavenly places (Luke 21.28; Eph. 4.30).

This redemption which was wrought by the death of Christ makes possible for us forgiveness of sins, a new relationship with God, a new life upon earth, and in the end the glory of heaven.

Now let us enquire what is implied in all these words which have to do with 'ransom', 'redemption', 'rescue', 'liberation'.

(i) They all imply that man was in captivity, in slavery, in subjection to an alien power. There was something which had man in its grip.

(ii) They all imply that by no conceivable means could man have effected his own liberation or rescue. He was helpless in the grip of a power and a situation which he could not mend and from which he could not break away.

(iii) His liberation was effected by the coming of Jesus Christ who paid the price which was necessary to achieve it.

(iv) Nowhere in the NT is there any word of to whom that price was paid. It could not have been paid to God because all the time God was so loving the world. It was in fact God's love that sent Christ into this world. It could not have been paid to the devil for that would put the devil on an equality with God. All that we can say is this—it cost the life and death of Christ to liberate man from the past, the present and the future power of sin. Beyond that we cannot go, but although thought may be baffled, experience shows that it cost the life of Jesus Christ to bring us home to God.

MAKROTHUMIA

THE DIVINE PATIENCE

THE noun *makrothumia* and the verb *makrothumein* are characteristically biblical words. They do not occur in classical Greek at all, and only very seldom in later Greek. They are indeed characteristically *Christian* words, for, as we shall see, they describe a Christian virtue which to the Greek was no virtue at all. In the NT *makrothumia* occurs fourteen times and *makrothumein* ten times. The AV varies between 'long-suffering' and 'patience'. These words have two uses.

(i) They describe the 'steadfast spirit which will never give in'. It is that spirit of 'patience' and faith which will ultimately inherit the promise. It was because Abraham 'patiently endured' that he in the end received the promise (Heb. 6.15). 'Patience' is a virtue that the Christian must have as he waits for the Day of the Lord, and he may learn it from the 'patience' of the farmer as he waits for the crop, and from the 'patience' of the prophets who never gave up their hope in God (Jas. 5.7-10). On this I Mac. (8.4) has a very illuminating use of the word. In that passage, as Trench points out, the Roman supremacy over all the world is ascribed to the Roman 'policy and patience'. And by that is meant, 'the Roman persistency which would never make peace under defeat'. The Christian must have this *makrothumia* which can endure delay and bear suffering and never give in.

(ii) They describe the 'attitude that a man should have towards his fellow-men'. This is the typically NT use of the words. Chrysostom defined *makrothumia* as the spirit which could take revenge if it liked, but utterly refuses to do so. Lightfoot explained it as the spirit which will never retaliate. Now this is the very opposite of Greek virtue. The great Greek virtue was *megalopsuchia*, which Aristotle defined as the refusal to tolerate any insult or injury. To the Greek the big man was the man who went all out for vengeance. To the Christian the big man is the man who, even when he can, refuses to do so.

(*a*) This patience with men is the characteristic of the 'Christian minister'. It is that very quality which Paul claims to be the proof of real apostleship (II Cor. 6.6, cp. I Tim. 1.16; II Tim. 3.10). No one can ever lead and guide and direct a Christian congregation without this patience, this *makrothumia*.

(*b*) It is the characteristic of the 'Christian preacher' (Tit. 2.2). Without it the preacher would be driven to pessimistic despair and to that irritability which wrecks preaching.

(*c*) It ought to be the characteristic of 'every Christian', 'every Church member'. It is included in the fruit of the Spirit (Gal. 5.22). Without it men cannot walk worthily of their Christian calling (Eph. 4.2; Col. 3.12). It must be exercised towards all men (I Thess. 5.14). It is one of the great characteristics of love (I Cor. 13.4). There can be no such thing as a Christian fellowship without *makrothumia*.

(iii) And the reason for that is just this—that *makrothumia* is the great characteristic of God (Rom. 2.4; 9.22).

It was God's *makrothumia* which delayed in the days of Noah until the ark was built (I Pet. 3.20). It is that very *makrothumia* which is responsible for man's salvation (II Pet. 3.9, 15). If God had been a man He would long ago have taken His hand and, with a gesture, would have wiped out the world, but in His 'patience' He bears with the sins, the follies and the disobedience of men.

The great obligation which rests on the Christian is just this—he must be as patient with his fellow-men as God has been with him.

MESITĒS

THE ONE BETWEEN

Mesitēs is one of the great NT titles of Jesus. It is usually translated 'mediator'. It comes from the Greek word *mesos*, which, in this instance, means 'in the middle', and *mesitēs* therefore means 'a man who stands in the middle and who brings two parties together'. In the NT it is used in Gal. 3.19 of Moses, and in I Tim. 2.5; Heb. 8.6; 9.15; 12.24 of Jesus. It was just such a person for whom Job's whole soul cried out in his misfortune, when he said of himself and God, 'Neither is there any daysman, *mesitēs*, between us' (Job 9.33).

In classical Greek the word itself is not common, but the idea is very common. When it and its equivalents appear, they have two main meanings.

(i) They mean an 'arbiter'. Both Greek and Roman law believed strongly in arbitration. In Athens there was a body of men called The Forty, who were made up of four from each of the ten tribes. People who had disputes brought them to The Forty, and The Forty appointed an arbiter or mediator to settle them. The arbiters were composed of every Athenian citizen in his sixtieth year. An arbiter could not refuse the task if selected, and it was his duty, at all costs, to effect a settlement and a reconciliation between two parties who were at variance. In Rome there was a body of men called the *arbitri*. When a case was a matter of pure law it was tried by a judge, *judex*, but when it was a matter of equity, for instance, a matter of damages incurred or the like, it was settled by an 'arbiter', whose duty it was to bring the dispute to an end. An arbiter, a mediator, a *mesitēs*, is therefore fundamentally a person whose duty it is to bring together two people who are estranged and to wipe out the differences between them. That is what Jesus did between us and God.

(ii) They mean 'a sponsor', 'a guarantor', 'a surety'. A man who went bail for another person's appearance in court was so called. But the words are specially used of guaranteeing or standing surety for a debt. If a man wished to borrow from a bank he had to find someone to stand guarantor, a *mesitēs*. The *mesitēs* was a man who was ready to pay his friend's debt. Jesus is the *mesitēs* who stands good for our debt to God.

Always the *mesitēs* is the person in the middle who brings two people together. The Jews regularly used the term of Moses. In the Assumption of Moses (1.14) Moses is made to say of God, 'He designed and devised me, and he prepared me before the foundation of the world, that I should be the mediator of his covenant.' It was Moses who was the connecting link between Israel and God. In later times the Jews believed that the prayers of men were borne to God by angels. The Testament of Dan (6.2) says, 'Draw near unto God and unto the angel who intercedeth for you, for he is a mediator between God and man.' The Christian needs no human and no angelic mediator. Christ is for him the connecting link with God.

So when we call Jesus *mesitēs*, 'mediator', we remember three great things.

(i) Jesus is God's intermediary. He is the connecting link between God and man. He is the King's messenger, the one who stands between God and man, not to separate them, but to bring them together.

(ii) The great function of the mediator is to bring together people who are at variance. Again and again the papyri speak of the appointment of a *mesitēs* to effect an agreement between people who are estranged. It is

Jesus' work to break down the barrier between God and man.

(iii) If a mediator is to be effective, he must perfectly represent both parties. Irenaeus described Jesus thus, *hominibus ostendens deum, deo autem exhibens hominem,* that is, He showed God to men and exhibited men to God. The very word shows us the great mystery of Christ, that at one and the same time He is perfectly God and perfectly man. That is why He, and He alone, is the only mediator between God and man.

PAIDAGŌGOS

THE GUARDIAN OF CHILDHOOD'S DAYS

THE word *paidagōgos* occurs in the NT in only two passages; but it is a word the correct understanding of which is essential, if Paul's thought is to be understood. In I Cor. 4.15 Paul says to the Corinthians that they may have ten thousand *paidagōgoi,* but they have not many fathers; that it is he who is their true father in the Christian faith. There, the AV translates the word 'instructors'; Moffatt translates 'thousands to superintend'; the RSV translates 'guides'. In Gal. 3.24, 25 the AV says that the law was our 'schoolmaster' (*paidagōgos*) to lead us to Christ . . . but after faith comes we are no longer under a *paidagōgos.* There Moffatt translates the law 'held us as wards in discipline'. And the RSV has it that the law was our 'custodian'. None of these translations is fully satisfactory, for the very good reason that the *paidagōgos* carried out a function to which there is nothing precisely corresponding in our educational system.

Up to the age of seven the Greek boy was almost exclusively in his mother's charge. But even then, if there was a *paidagōgos* in the household, he had his say. Socrates in Plato's *Protagoros* (325 c) says of the child: 'Mother and nurse and father and *paidagōgos* are quarrelling about the improvement of the child as soon as ever he is able to understand them.' It was when he went to school that the *paidagōgos* really took over the management of the boy and retained it till the boy was eighteen. The *paidagōgos* was not in our sense of the word a teacher at all. His duty was to accompany the boy to school each day and to see that he got there safely; to carry the boy's books and his lyre; to watch his conduct in school; to see to his conduct in the street; to train the boy in morals, in manners and in deportment. He must see that the boy walked modestly with downcast head in the streets; he must see that he gave place to older people and was becomingly silent in their presence; he must teach him to be well-mannered at table and to wear his clothes with grace. He had to teach him all the Greek meant by *eukosmia*, good manners, good deportment, pleasantness of life. K. J. Freeman says of the *paidagōgos* that he was 'a mixture of nurse, footman, chaperon and tutor'. When in the *Lysis* (208 c) Socrates is trying to teach the lad that life does not consist in doing what you like there is a conversation like this. 'Are you your own master, or do they not even allow that?' 'Nay; of course they do not allow that.' 'Then you have a master?' 'Yes, my *paidagōgos*; there he is.' . . . 'And what does he do with you?' 'He takes me to my teachers.' It was an anxious and a most practical job, especially if the lad was a high-spirited and independent boy. Plato compares the relationship of the *paidagōgos* to his charge to that of an invalid to his health: 'He has to follow the disease wherever it leads, being unable to cure it, and he spends his life in perpetual anxiety with no time for anything else' (Plato: *Republic*, 406 a). Clement of Alexandria has a work called *The Paedagogus* in which he likens the Word to our *paidagōgos*. He says: 'The *paidagōgos* being practical, not theoretical, his aim is thus to improve the soul, and to train it up to a virtuous, not to an intellectual life'. Plutarch in his life of Quintus Fabius Cunctator tells how Fabius defeated Hannibal. He refused to join in battle but he dogged Hannibal's armies everywhere. 'Still he kept pace with them; when they marched he followed them; when they encamped he did the same.' There were those who wished for violent action and they taunted Fabius with being Hannibal's *paidagōgos*, 'since he did nothing else but follow him up and down and wait upon him' (Plutarch, *Life of Fabius* 5). Clearly the *paidagōgos* had a most constant and a most responsible task.

But here we have the very point of the matter. Sometimes the slave chosen to be *paidagōgos* was old and trusted. Sometimes he had the highest ideal of his task. It is told of a good *paidagōgos* that, when he was asked, 'What is your duty?' he replied, 'My duty is to make the good pleasant to the boy.' When Themistocles wished to send to Xerxes the secret massage which lured him to his doom it was to Sikinnos, the *paidagōgos* of his sons, that he entrusted it, and afterwards rewarded him with wealth and the citizenship (*Herodotus* 8.75). Sometimes indeed the *paidagōgos* was the trusted family friend. But far oftener the *paidagōgos* was a most unsatisfactory figure. Far too often he was chosen for his task, as Plutarch complains, because he was too old and feeble for any other.

Pericles is reported to have said when he saw a slave fall from a tree and break his leg: 'Lo, he is now a *paidagōgos*!' In Plato's *Alcibiades* (122 b) Socrates says to Alcibiades: 'Pericles gave you, Alcibiades, for a *paidagōgos* Zopyrus, the Thracian, a slave of his who was past all other work.' At the very end of Plato's *Lysis* the *paidagōgoi* arrive to take Lysis and Menexenus home. The conversation is not ended and the lads are unwilling to go. Plato goes on: 'Suddenly we were interrupted by the *paidagōgoi* of Lysis and Menexenus, who came upon us like an evil apparition with the lads' brothers, and bade them go home as it was getting late. At first we and the bystanders drove them off; but afterwards, as they paid no attention, but only went on shouting in their barbarous dialect, and got angry and kept calling the boys—they seemed to us to have been drinking rather too much at the Hermaea, which made them difficult to manage—we fairly gave way and broke up the company.' It is not a pretty picture, the picture of uncouth, drunken slaves with no pretensions either to morals or to culture. It is true that the other side sometimes appears. In a third century papyrus a mother writes to her son: 'Let you and your *paidagōgos* see to it that you go to a fitting teacher,' and she ends the letter, 'Salute your much honoured *paidagōgos*, Eros.' But the balance is very much the other way.

In any event the *paidagōgos* existed for no other reason than to make his charge independent of his care. Xenophon in his work on Sparta (3.1) writes: 'Whenever they emerge from childhood to youth, they cease from *paidagōgoi*, they cease from teachers. No one governs them any more, but they let them go as masters of themselves.' When Paul spoke of the law as our *paidagōgos* to bring us to Christ, in the very phrase he affirmed that the law was an inadequate, unsatisfactory thing, doomed to come to an end. It was another way of saying that Christ is the end of the law.

PAROUSIA

THE ARRIVAL OF THE KING

THE Greek word *parousia* has become naturalized in English as a technical term for the Second Coming of Christ. The use of the word in the secular Greek contemporary with the NT is extremely interesting.

(i) In classical Greek it means quite simply the 'presence' or the 'arrival' of persons or things. It can be used in such phrases as the 'presence' of friends or the 'presence' of misfortunes. A man takes an oath that he will fulfil a certain duty in the presence of the brothers and the bishops. Quite often Paul uses *parousia* in that simple non-technical sense. He rejoices at the *parousia*, the 'arrival' of Stephanas (I Cor. 16.17). He is comforted by the *parousia* of Titus (II Cor. 7.6). He urges the Philippians to be as obedient in his absence as they were during his *parousia* with them (Phil. 2.12). The Corinthians fling the taunt at him that, however impressive his letters may be, his bodily *parousia*, presence, is weak (II Cor. 10.10).

(ii) But, characteristically, in the NT *parousia* is the word for the Second Coming of Christ (Matt. 24.3, 27, 37, 39;

I Thess. 2.19; 3.13; 4.15; 5.23; II Thess. 2.1, 8, 9; Jas. 5.7, 8; II Pet. 1.16; 3.4, 12; I John 2.28). Let us study the contemporary secular use of the term to see what kind of picture it would convey to the minds of the early Christians.

In the papyri and in hellenistic Greek *parousia* is the technical word for the arrival of an emperor, a king, a governor or famous person into a town or province. For such a visit preparations have to be made. Taxes are imposed, for instance, to present the king with a golden crown. For the visit of Ptolemy Soter to the village of Cerceosiris 80 artabae of corn have to be collected. Always the coming of the king demands that all things must be ready.

Further, one of the commonest things is that provinces dated a new era from the *parousia* of the emperor. Cos dated a new era from the *parousia* of Gaius Caesar in A.D. 4, as did Greece from the *parousia* of Hadrian in A.D. 124. A new section of time emerged with the coming of the king.

Another common practice was to strike new coins to commemorate the visitation of the king. Hadrian's travels can be followed by the coins which were struck to commemorate his visits. When Nero visited Corinth coins were struck to commemorate his *adventus*, advent, which is the Latin equivalent of the Greek *parousia*. It was as if with the coming of the king a new set of values had emerged.

Parousia is sometimes used of the 'invasion' of a province by a general. It is so used of the invasion of Asia by Mithradates. It describes the entrance on the scene of a new and conquering power.

Lastly, *parousia* is used of the visitation of a god. It is used, for instance, of the visit of the god to a sufferer, who was healed, in the temple of Aesculapius, the god of healing. On the political side, the *parousia* of the king or governor or emperor was often an occasion when petitions were presented and wrongs were righted. The word describes a healing and a correcting visitation.

With all this in our minds let us return to the NT and see how the idea of the *parousia* is used.

(i) It is used as the basis of a demand to preserve life blameless against the coming of the king. The preparations must be made (I Thess. 3.13; 5.23; I John 2.28).

(ii) It is used as a reason for patience (Jas. 5.7, 8). The day is coming when the coming of the King will right all wrongs.

(iii) It is spoken of as something to desire and to pray for (II Pet. 3.4, 12). R. L. Stevenson tells of a byreman, who said that he never wearied of his unattractive work because 'he that has something ayont (beyond) need never weary'. He who awaits Christ has the something beyond.

Deissmann says that the word precisely expresses the text, 'Behold, thy King cometh unto thee' (Zech. 9.9; Matt. 21.5). The Christian is one who awaits a king.

PHOBOS

THE RIGHT AND THE WRONG FEAR

Phobos means 'fear', and in all ages of Greek *phobos* is what is sometimes known as 'a middle word'. That is to say, the word itself is quite neutral, and, according to the way in which it is used and the context in which it occurs, it can have either a good or a bad meaning, and can describe something which is useful and praiseworthy, or evil and contemptible. In Greek *phobos*, 'fear' can be the characteristic either of the coward or of the truly religious man.

In classical Greek *phobos* has three main meanings. (i) In Homer it nearly always means 'panic' or 'flight'. 'Panic-stricken flight,' says Homer, 'which is the companion of chilling *phobos*, fear' (*Iliad*, 9.2). *Phobos* in early Greek has always in it the idea of running away, of fleeing panic-stricken from the battle. The passive of the corresponding verb, *phobeisthai*, means 'to be put to flight', and it is the opposite of the verb *hupomenein*, from which comes *hupomonē*, and which means 'to stand fast' and 'to endure'. The word has in it that failure of nerve which makes a man take to his heels and flee. (ii) More generally in classical Greek *phobos* means 'fear' in the widest sense of the term. It is the opposite of *tharros*, which means 'courage'. (iii) Lastly, in classical Greek, *phobos* means 'awe' or 'reverence' for some exalted ruler and especially for some divinity or some god. It is the feeling which a man experiences in the presence of someone who is infinitely his superior.

In the NT the word is common and occurs about 47 times. First of all, let us look at it in the Synoptic Gospels and in Acts.

It is used of the reaction of the disciples when they saw Jesus walking on the water (Matt. 14.26) and when He stilled the storm (Mark 4.41). It is used of the reaction of the people after the healing of the paralysed man (Luke 5.26), after the raising of the widow's son at Nain (Luke 7.16), after the healing of the Gerasene demoniac (Luke 8.37). It is used of the feeling of Zacharias when he saw the angel of the Lord beside the altar (Luke 1.12), and of the spectators when Zacharias recovered his speech (Luke 1.65). It is used of the shepherds when they heard the song of the angels (Luke 2.9). It is used of the guards at the tomb when the angel rolled the stone away (Matt. 28.4), and of the women as they went home after seeing the empty tomb (Matt. 28.8). It is used of the feelings of men in the midst of the shattering events of the last days (Luke 21.26).

In Acts it is used of the feeling in men's minds when they saw the signs and wonders and felt the power in the early Church (Acts 2.43). It is used of the reaction of the people after the death of Ananias and Sapphira (Acts 5.5, 11). It is used of the discomfited heathen exorcists at Ephesus (Acts 19.17). The Church is said to walk in the *phobos*, the 'fear', of the Lord (Acts 9.31).

In not one case in the Synoptic Gospels or Acts is *phobos* used in a bad sense. In every case it describes the feeling in a man's heart when he is confronted with the divine power in action. It always describes the feelings of a man when he finds himself in the presence of what Otto called 'the wholly other', when he finds himself face to face with something outside and beyond and different from himself, something which he cannot understand.

There is here the truth that there can be no religion without reverence. Between man and God there is 'intimacy' but not 'familiarity'. It describes the feeling of the man who is 'lost in wonder, love and praise'. It describes that awe which comes upon the creature in the presence of the Creator. In a famous sentence Swinburne wrote: 'Glory to man in the highest, for man is the master of things.' *Phobos* is the very opposite of that, for, in its highest sense, *phobos* is the essential reverence of man in the presence of God.

In the rest of the NT the word *phobos* is a much more complicated word. It can have both a good and a bad sense. Let us start with the good sense.

(i) In many cases the word 'fear' translates *phobos* in the AV where the meaning is rather 'reverence' than 'fear'. We have already seen that in Acts 9.31 it is said the Churches were 'walking in the fear of the Lord', that is, the Christians were living reverent lives. It is Paul's condemnation of the heathen world that there is no 'fear of God' before their eyes (Rom. 3.18). Reverence, respect for God, was entirely lacking. Peter talks about passing the time of your sojourning here 'in fear' (I Pet. 1.17). A man must be ready to give a reason for his hope in meekness and 'fear' (I Pet. 3.15). In this sense *phobos* describes the feeling of the man who is living in the shadow of eternity, who is always conscious of God, who never forgets that he will give account for the things he does.

(ii) This *phobos*, this 'reverence', this 'awareness' of God, is the source of certain great things. It is the source of 'the chaste life' (I Pet. 3.2). This awareness of God necessarily exercises an antiseptic influence on life.

(iii) This *phobos* is the source of 'holiness' (II Cor. 7.1). Because God is holy, God's man must be holy too. There must be a difference in the Christian life and that difference finds its motive power and mainspring in the sense of God.

(iv) This *phobos* is connected with the 'godly sorrow' that brings repentance (II Cor. 7.11). Repentance must have as one of its roots the feeling of inadequacy, of failure, of unworthiness in the presence of the holy perfection of God. That feeling produces in the first instance *phobos*, the sense of abasement of the creature in the presence of the Creator.

(v) This *phobos* is the source of Christian effort (Phil. 2.12). The Christian must work out his own salvation with *phobos*, 'fear', and trembling. The sense of the judgment which he faces, the sense of the goal which he may miss, the sense of the crucial importance of life and living, the sense of the necessity of in some way seeking to deserve the love of Christ, all combine to fill the Christian with an awed wonder and a trembling eagerness, and a passionate effort.

(vi) This *phobos* is the basis of the 'mutual respect' and 'mutual service' which Christians are bound to render to each other (Eph. 5.21). All Christians live in the presence of God. All must be conscious, not only of their own salvation, but also of the brother for whom Christ died. Christians, because of their common reverence for God, also reverence each other.

(vii) This *phobos* can be 'the motive power of persuasion' (II Cor. 5.11). It is because he knows the *phobos* of God that Paul seeks to persuade the Corinthians. It is altogether wrong completely to excise the threat from the Christian message. Christianity always comes to men with a promise and an offer, but any promise can be disbelieved and any offer can be refused, and there is a necessary consequence of refusal and disbelief.

(viii) The Pastoral Epistles have one rather special instance of *phobos*. Christian discipline is to be publicly exercised that others may see it and 'fear' (I Tim. 5.20). It is an interesting thought that Christian discipline is to be exercised not only for the sake of the man who has sinned, but also as a means of warning the man who has not sinned to abide in the right way.

It can easily be seen that NT thought traces many of the greatest things to this *phobos*, this 'reverence', this constant 'awareness' of the presence of God.

We may now turn to the other side of *phobos*, the side in which *phobos* is an evil thing.

(i) Before we turn to the really bad side of *phobos* we

must look at two things which are not bad in themselves, but which could become bad. *Phobos* describes the 'natural shrinking' from some difficult task. So Paul uses *phobos* of his own feelings regarding the unhappy situation in the Church at Corinth (I Cor. 2.3; II Cor. 7.5). Such a *phobos* is natural and inevitable. The more sensitive a man is the more acutely it will come to him. In itself it is nothing to be ashamed of, but it becomes a bad thing if it stops a man doing what he knows he ought to do and facing what he knows he ought to face.

(ii) *Phobos* is used of the feeling of 'respect' a man should have in the presence of human authority. The Corinthians received Titus with *phobos* (II Cor. 7.15). The NT repeatedly enjoins that those who are in positions of authority in the State and the Church must receive the *phobos* which is their due (Rom. 13.7; Eph. 6.5; I Pet. 2.18). But it is to be noted that this respect must never become subservience. Caesar must always receive his things, and God must always receive His.

(iii) And now we come to the definitely bad side of *phobos*. There is a *phobos* which is characteristically the bad man's emotion (Rom. 13.3). In the face of authority the upright man has nothing to fear. *Phobos* is the child of evil-doing.

(iv) There is the *phobos*, the 'fear', of dying (Heb. 2.15). An American journalist set high in the list of his personal rules for life, 'Never to allow myself to think of death.' It was Dr. Johnson who declared that the fear of death was so naturally ingrained into man that life was one long effort to keep it at bay. That is a *phobos* from which the Christian hope must deliver a man. The Christian cannot be haunted by the fear of death.

(v) *Phobos* and legalism go hand in hand. Legalism reduces a man to being a slave instead of a son, and the characteristic feeling of the slave is *phobos*, 'fear' (Rom. 8.15). It was Paul's belief that a religion dominated by law cannot issue in anything else but fear. But the Christian holds a faith dominated by grace, in which he is a son of love and not a slave of law.

(vi) The cure for *phobos*, 'fear', is love (I John 4.16, 18). Perfect love ejects fear from life. Fear, said John, has torment (I John 4.18). Fear has to do with punishment, but Christianity teaches us to think not so much of the vengeance as of the love of God, not so much of the punishment as of the forgiveness of God.

When we put that saying of Paul and that saying of John together we get a very interesting and suggestive thought. Together they go to prove that fear is the sign of an inadequate religion. When fear becomes the motive power of religion it means that a man is thinking of religion in terms of law and of God in terms of vengeance. In Christianity there is both law and judgment, but when they become so dominant that they oust grace and love from a man's thoughts they issue in an inadequate religion.

(vii) *Phobos*, 'fear', is the cowardice which prevents a man from bearing the Christian witness he ought to bear. This is a characteristic usage of the Fourth Gospel. Fear of the Jews kept men from confessing their faith in Jesus (John 7.13). It made Joseph of Arimathaea remain a secret disciple (John 19.38). It kept the disciples terrified and behind locked doors after the crucifixion (John 20.19). It is that which may prevent a man in time of trouble from showing whose he is and whom he serves (I Pet. 3.14). *Phobos* destroys the essential heroism of the Christian faith.

In the NT *phobos* is one of the great words. There can be no religion at all without the awe of the creature in the presence of the Creator. The feeling of reverence, the awareness of God, is at once the prophylactic against sin, the dynamic of the Christian life, and the mainspring of Christian effort. But when reverence turns to fear in the lower sense of the term then religion becomes a stunted and inadequate thing, which, because it has lost its grace, has lost its glory.

PLEONEXIA

THE SIN OF GREED

Pleonexia is a sin which the NT again and again most unsparingly condemns. The word occurs in Mark 7.22; Luke

12.15; Rom. 1.29; II Cor. 9.5; Eph. 4.19; 5.3; Col. 3.5; I Thess. 2.5; II Pet. 2.3, 14. The regular AV translation is 'covetousness'. Once, in Eph. 4.19, the AV translates it 'greediness'. The RSV retains 'covetousness' in most passages but translates 'greedy practice' in Eph. 4.5 and 'greed' in the II Pet. passages. Moffatt varies more. He retains 'covetousness' in Luke 12.15, but his regular translation is 'lust', which he uses in seven of the passages. Once, in I Thess. 2.5, he uses 'self-seeking'.

Pleonexia in all ages of Greek is an ugly word, and always it has a certain basic idea behind it which none of the translations wholly bring out, because it cannot be brought out in any one word. In classical Greek it means 'an arrogant greediness', the spirit which tries to take advantage of its fellow-men. The corresponding verb, *pleonektein*, means 'to defraud' or 'overreach'. Polybius, the Greek historian, has one suggestive use of the word. The Stoics had a phrase by which they described 'that which is fitting'—*ta kathēkonta*—by which they meant that kind of conduct which a good man ought to produce. Polybius says that the man who is guilty of this covetous conduct uses methods which are not fitting for a man to use. *Pleonexia* was a word which was much in the vocabulary of the ordinary people and it is common in the papyri. There it is connected with conduct which is 'quite shameless', with 'overreaching ambition', with 'violence', with 'injustice', with the 'cupidity' for which a man in his better moments will be sorry, with the 'rapacity' of a dishonest official who is out to fleece the district of which he is in charge. By the Latin moralists it is defined as *amor sceleratus habendi*, 'the accursed love of possessing'. Theodoret, the early commentator, describes it as 'the aiming always at getting more, the snatching at things which it does not befit a man to have'. Cicero defined *avaritia*, which is the Latin equivalent, as *injuriosa appetitio alienorum*, 'the unlawful desire for things which belong to others'.

Now let us see if we can classify the NT usages so that we may arrive at the basic quality of this sin.

(i) In Rom. 1.29 *pleonexia* is the sin of the godless world.

It is the sin of the world, of the society, of the man who has turned his back upon the laws of God. It is the very opposite of the generosity of the love of God and of the charity of the Christian life.

(ii) In Luke 12.15 it is the sin of the man who evaluates life in material terms, who thinks that the value of life lies in the number of things that a man possesses, the man whose one desire is to get and who never even thinks of giving.

(iii) In I Thess. 2.5 and in II Pet. 2.3 it describes the sin of the man who uses his position to take advantage of, 'to make merchandise of' the people he ought to serve, the man who sees his fellow-men as creatures to be exploited and not as sons of God to be served.

(iv) In Col. 3.5 it is identified with idolatry. *Pleonexia* is the worship of things instead of God. A threepenny-piece is a little thing, yet if it is held before the eye it will blot out the vastness of the sun. When a man has *pleonexia* in his heart he loses sight of God in a mad desire to get.

(v) In passage after passage it is connected with sexual sin (Mark 7.22; Rom. 1.29; Eph. 4.19; 5.3; II Pet. 2.14). Here is the very essence of the word. The essence is not the sexual sin. The essence is the desire to have what is forbidden, the desire to take what should not be taken, the giving of rein to appetites and desires which are against the laws of God and man.

Lightfoot (on Rom. 1.29)) defines *pleonexia* as 'the disposition which is ever ready to sacrifice one's neighbour to oneself in all things, not in money dealings merely'. *Pleonexia* is the sin of the man who has allowed full play to the desire to have what he should not have, who thinks that his desires and appetites and lusts are the most important thing in the world, who sees others as things to be exploited, who has no god except himself and his desires.

PŌROUN AND PŌRŌSIS

THE HARDENING OF THE HEART

Pōroun is the verb and *pōrōsis* is the noun which are used in the NT to express the idea of what the AV calls 'the hardening of the hearts of men'. These words are interesting, not only for their history, but also for a most suggestive shift of meaning which they undergo.

At the back of both of them there is the word *pōros*. *Pōros* is used in a variety of senses. Basically it means a kind of stone, which Theophrastus in his work on stones describes as a stone like Parian marble in colour and in texture but lighter. Aristotle used the word for a stalactite, one of these solidified droppings of water in a cavern. In the papyri the word is used of the kind of stone that is used to pack the foundation course of a building. Medically the words have certain technical uses. *Pōros* means the chalk stone that forms in the joints and paralyses action. It also means a stone in the bladder; and *pōrōsis* means the process by which a callus forms at the joining of the break when fractured bones unite. *Pōrōsis* does not mean a callus on the skin, as, for instance, a callus formed on the hand by digging; the Greek for that is *tulē*, which is not a NT word. *Pōrōsis* is the much harder and much more irremovable bone callus that forms when a fracture unites. In all these cases it is easy to see that the basic meaning of the word is an impenetrable hardness, a hardness like bone or even marble.

The words then acquire two different sets of meanings. (i) They are used in connection with something which has 'lost all power of sensation'. Athenaeus has a queer story of Dionysius of Heracles. He became overfat from overeating. He became subject to fits of coma. His surgeons could only arouse him by pricking him with long needles. And even then certain parts of his body had lost all power of feeling because the fat had lost its sense of feeling. It had become *pepōrōmenē*, which is the perfect participle passive of the verb *pōroun*. The words have now become definitely connected with 'loss of feeling'. (ii) The words become connected with the idea of 'blindness' and 'inability to see'. The word *pōroun* is the only one of the group which occurs in the Septuagint, and it only occurs once, in Job 17.7 there the AV has it: 'Mine eyes *have grown dim* by reason of sorrow.'

So then we may say that at the back of them this group of words has three ideas—the idea of 'hardness', the idea of 'lack of the power to feel', and the idea of 'blindness', lack of the power to see. With this background in our minds we turn to the NT.

Pōroun and *pōrōsis* together occur eight times in the NT.

(i) They describe the mental condition of a man 'who cannot see the lesson that events are designed to teach him'. In Mark 6.52 the disciples were bewildered when Jesus came to them walking on the water because they did not see the meaning of the miracle of the loaves and fishes, because their hearts were 'hardened' (*pepōrōmenē*). When they were crossing the lake, they were worried about the fact that they had forgotten to bring bread with them. This episode in Mark follows the feeding of the four thousand; and Jesus asked them why they were so worried about having no bread. 'Have you your hearts yet hardened?' He asks (*pepōrōmenē*) (Mark 8.17). The word here describes the blind insensitiveness which will not learn a lesson. We sometimes say that things make no 'impression' on a person. Now there were certain Greek thinkers who believed that things did literally make an 'impression' on the mind. It was as if words and sights and ideas impinged on the soft, wax-like substance of the mind, and literally left an 'impression'. But clearly if the mind becomes hardened there can be no such thing as an 'impression' on it. Here the word describes unteachability. It describes the man who is so wrapped up in his own little world that nothing from any other world can touch him, the man whose mind is shut to all ideas but his own, the man who is impervious to the lessons that events are designed to teach him.

(ii) They describe the mental condition of the man 'who

has made himself incapable of seeing the meaning of God's word for him'. Paul says of the Jews that their minds are 'blinded' when they hear the word of God read to them (II Cor. 3.14). A man can lose any faculty if he will not use it. Darwin lamented the fact that he had lost the power to appreciate music and poetry, because he had given all his time to biology. He said that if he had life to live over again he would keep that faculty of appreciation alive. If a man erects his ideas into supreme authority for long enough he will in the end be incapable of receiving the ideas of God.

(iii) They describe 'the attitude of the Jews' to God. In spite of the miracles they did not believe in Jesus because God had blinded their eyes and 'hardened' their hearts (John 12.40). These are the words that Paul twice uses to describe what had been happening to Israel throughout all her history (Rom. 11.7, 25). They describe the man who stubbornly takes his own way, who is deaf to the appeal of God, because he has been busy making God in his own image. They describe the man who thinks he knows better than God.

(iv) The immoralities of the Gentile world are due to the fact that their understandings were darkened because of the *pōrōsis* of their hearts (Eph. 4.18). The idea is that they have so long stifled conscience that conscience has ceased to function. Conscience has petrified. It is so calloused that it has no sensitiveness left.

(v) When Jesus was about to heal the man with the withered hand in the Synagogue and when he saw the bleak looks of the orthodox because the deed was going to be done on a Sabbath He was grieved at the 'hardness' (*pōrōsis*) of their hearts (Mark 3.5). There are two things there. (*a*) They had so long identified religion with rules and regulations that they could not recognize real religion when they saw it. (*b*) They had so legalized religion that they had forgotten human sympathy. Because they had so long taken their way and not God's way they were completely insensitive alike to the appeal of God and the appeal of human need.

Whenever a man sets his own ideas in the place that God should take, whenever he stubbornly goes his own way, he is on the way to a condition in which his heart is petrified, in which his heart and his conscience have become insensitive and when his eyes are blind.

PRAUS AND PRAOTĒS

CHRISTIAN GENTLENESS

THE word *praus* is the word which is used in the Beatitude which says, Blessed are the *meek* (Matt. 5.5). This adjective occurs three other times in the NT. Twice it is used of Jesus Himself (Matt. 11.29; 21.5). The other occasion is in I Pet. 3.4. The noun *praotēs* is the word which is used for 'meekness' in Paul's account of the fruit of the Spirit (Gal 5.23). Its other occurrences are I Cor. 4.21; II Cor. 10.1; Gal. 6.1; Eph. 4.2; Col. 3.12; II Tim. 2.25; Tit. 3.2; Jas. 1.21; 3.13; I Pet. 3.15. The AV without exception translates the adjective by 'meek' and the noun by 'meekness'. Moffatt has 'humble' in the Beatitude; 'modesty' in the James passages; and 'gentle' or 'gentleness' in all the others. He never retains the translation 'meek'. The American RSV has 'humble' once, in Matt. 21.5; 'meek' or 'meekness' five times, included among which is the Beatitude; and 'gentle' or 'gentleness' in the remaining passages.

In classical Greek this is a lovely word. Of things it means 'gentle'. It is used, for instance, of a gentle breeze or a gentle voice. Of persons it means 'mild' or 'gracious'. Menander has a fragment in which he says, 'How sweet is a father who is *mild* and young in heart.' It would be true to say that in classical Greek it is a word with a caress in it. Indeed Xenophon uses the neuter plural of the adjective in the sense of caresses. It is characteristically a kindly and a gracious word.

Aristotle discussed it. For Aristotle every virtue consisted in the mean which lies between the two extremes. He defined *praotēs* as the mean between *orgilotēs* and *aorgēsia*, that is to say, the mean between excessive anger and excessive angerlessness. He said that it was the secret of equanimity and composure. We might put it this way—the man who is *praus* is the man who is always angry at the right time and never angry at the wrong time.

That brings us to the use of *praus* which really illumines the whole matter. In Greek *praus* is used in one special sense. It is used—as is *mitis* in Latin—for a beast which has been tamed. A horse which was once wild but which has become obedient to the bit and to the bridle is *praus*.

Now herein lies the secret of the meaning of *praus*. There is gentleness in *praus* but behind the gentleness there is the strength of steel, for the supreme characteristic of the man who is *praus* is that he is the man who is under perfect control. It is not a spineless gentleness, a sentimental fondness, a passive quietism. It is a strength under control. Num. 12.3 tells us that Moses was the 'meekest' man upon the earth, but that same Moses was a man who could act with decision and blaze with anger when the occasion arose.

To such a character no man can attain by himself and his own efforts. *Praotēs* is strength under control, but it would be wrong to say that the man who is *praus* is perfectly *self*-controlled. He is perfectly *God*-controlled, for only God can give him that perfect mastery. It should be our prayer that God will make us *praus*, masters of ourselves, for only then can we be the servants of others.

PROSAGEIN AND PROSAGŌGĒ

THE WORD OF INTRODUCTION

THE verb *prosagein* means 'to bring to', and the noun *prosagōgē* means 'a way of entrance, access' or 'introduction'. Together they are used eight times in the NT, and of these eight times four have reference to the work of Jesus for men. On four occasions the word *prosagein* is used in a quite ordinary way. In Matt. 18.24 it is used of 'bringing' the debtor into the presence of the master. In Luke 9.41 it is the word that Jesus uses when He commands the epileptic boy to be 'brought' to him. In Acts 16.20 it is used of 'bringing' Paul and Silas into the presence of the magistrates at Philippi. In Acts 27.27 it is used of land 'drawing near' during the storm. *Prosagein* is used once of the special work of Jesus. In I Pet. 3.18 it is said that Christ died that He might 'bring' us to God. *Prosagōgē* is always used in the NT of the work of Jesus. In Eph. 2.18 it is said that through Him we both, Jew and Gentile, have 'access' to the Father. In Eph. 3.12 it is said that in Jesus we have boldness and 'access' to God with confidence. And in Rom. 5.2 it is said that through Jesus we have 'access' by faith into this grace in which we stand.

The great interest of these words, when they are used of the work of Jesus, comes from the many pictures which lie behind them.

(i) *Prosagein* is used in the Septuagint of bringing sacrificial victims to God (Lev. 3.12; 4.4; 8.14). It is the word which is used of bringing to God something which is especially dedicated to His use and His service.

(ii) *Prosagein* is used in the Septuagint for bringing chosen men into the presence of God that they may be ordained as priests for His worship and His service (Ex. 29.4).

(iii) In the heathen world in the time of the NT many people found their way closer to God in the Mystery Religions than through any other of the pagan faiths. The Mystery Religions were like passion plays which the worshipper was only allowed to see after a long period of preparation. After this period he became an initiate. When he did become an initiate, he was brought into the presence of the sacred mysteries by a person called the *mustagōgos*, and the technical word for 'bringing him in' is *prosagein*. The word describes the bringing of someone into the presence of something specially sacred and holy.

(iv) In secular Greek *prosagein* is regularly used of 'introducing' a speaker into the presence of the *dēmos*, the assembly of the people, or into the *boulē*, the senate or council. It is regularly used of 'introducing' ambassadors to the assembly of the people when they came to seek terms; and it is regularly used of 'bringing a person into' a court of justice and before a judge. *Prosagein* is then the word which is used of introducing a person into the presence of some higher authority.

(v) But *prosagein* has a very special usage. It is specially used of 'introducing a person into the presence of a king'. Xenophon tells how prisoners in chains were 'brought into the presence' of Cyrus the king (Xenophon, *Cyropaedia* 3.2.12). He tells how Cyrus expected anyone who wanted anything from him to get into favour with his friends and, through them, to ask for a *prosagōgē*, 'an introduction to the royal presence' (*Cyropaedia* 7.5.45). He tells how Sacas, the cup-bearer, had the office of 'introducing' (*prosagein*) to Astyages those who had business with him, and of keeping out those whom he thought it not expedient to admit (*Cyropaedia* 1.3.8). There was, in fact, an official at the Persian court called the *prosagōgeus*, the introducer, whose function it was to introduce people into the royal presence.

Every single use of these words lights up the work that Jesus does for men. Jesus is the person who introduces us into the royal presence of God. With Him alone we can enter into that presence without fear, He is God's introducer. When He introduces us to that presence He introduces us to the supreme authority for our lives; He introduces us into the presence of the holiest and the most sacred of all; He introduces us that, through Him, we may dedicate our lives as a sacrifice to the service of God. Can we think of Jesus better than as the one who 'introduces' us into the presence of God that we may receive God's grace and give to God our willing service?

There remains one special use of *prosagōgē* at which we must look. In Rom. 5.2 we read that through Jesus we have 'access', *prosagōgē*, into the grace in which we stand. Now *prosagōgē*, when it means 'access' or 'introduction', is always used of introduction to 'persons', therefore this use is slightly different. In hellenistic Greek *prosagōgē* is used of 'a place for ships to put in'. Plutarch speaks of a general who drew up his troops on terrain in front of the sea where there was no *prosagōgē*, no place for ships to put in (*Aemilius* 13). In Sophocles (*Philoctetes* 236) we find the phrase, 'What need made you put in (*prosagein*) to Lemnos?' The likelihood is that in this Romans passage *prosagōgē* is used in this sense, and that the phrase means, 'Jesus opened to us a way into the haven of God's grace.' The idea is that we are storm-tossed by sin and sorrow and trouble and temptation, and Jesus offers us the way into the harbour, the haven, the shelter of God's grace. We are like storm-tossed mariners who would make shipwreck of life unless Jesus took over the piloting of the ship of life and steered it out of the storm into the safe haven of the grace of God.

PROSLAMBANESTHAI

THE WORD OF WELCOME

Proslambanesthai is a verb which means 'to lay hold on, or to take to oneself'. In the NT it occurs eleven times. In Matt. 16.22 and Mark 8.32 it is used of Peter 'laying hold' of Jesus when Jesus first foretold His coming death. In Acts 27.33 it is used of 'taking food'. In Acts 17.5 it is used of the Thessalonian Jews 'laying hold of', or 'enlisting the help of' the corner-boys of Thessalonica to cause a riot against Paul and his company. In Acts 28.2 it is used of the people of Malta 'receiving' Paul and the ship's company when they were shipwrecked. These usages are perfectly straightforward. It is the remaining instances which are of special interest.

In Acts 18.26 *proslambanesthai* is used of Aquila and Priscilla 'taking Apollos to themselves' in order to explain the Christian way more fully to him. In Rom. 14.1 Paul uses it of 'receiving' into the fellowship of the Church the brother who is weak in the faith; and in Rom. 14.3 Paul says that God has 'received' us. In Rom. 15.7 Paul uses it when he says that all Christians ought 'to receive' one another. And in Philem. 17 he uses it when he urges

Philemon 'to receive' the runaway slave Onesimus as he would have received Paul himself. From these usages we see that *proslambanesthai* is an almost technical word for 'receiving someone into the Christian Church and fellowship and faith'.

Let us see the flavour of the word so that we can perhaps understand a little more fully what that Christian reception ought to mean.

(i) In the Septuagint *proslambanesthai* is often used of the way in which God receives His people. In Ps. 27.10 the Psalmist says that when his father and mother abandon him the Lord 'will take him up'. In Ps. 65.4 the Psalmist sings of the happiness of the man whom God chooses and 'takes to Himself'. In I Sam. 12.22 it is used when Samuel says that the Lord has graciously 'taken Israel to Himself' for a people. Here, then, is the first thing this word tells us. When we receive others we should receive them as God receives them. The same word is used for God's reception of His people and the Christian's reception of his fellow-man. In our welcome to others there must be all the generosity, the forgiveness, the sheer kindness of God.

(ii) In classical Greek it is used widely and regularly of 'taking someone to oneself as a helper'. It is used by Xenophon of a leader who receives as his helpers a new force of cavalry and infantry. He uses it of a leader who brings cities into alliance with himself either with or against their will. It is particularly used with three Greek words. It is used with *summachos,* which means 'an ally', with *sunergos,* which means a 'fellow-labourer', and with *koinōnos,* which means 'a partner in a business'. When we receive someone into the Church and the Christian fellowship we receive him as 'an ally' and a 'helper'. That means two things. (*a*) For us, it means that we must never receive anyone into the Christian fellowship without an honest attempt to see how his gifts may best be used for the good of the fellowship. The Church is full of people with gifts which have never been used. (*b*) For the person received, it means that he must enter the Christian fellowship, not with a view to resting back and doing nothing, but with a view to bringing all his strength and talents to bear on the Christian campaign. The Church is equally full of people who have gifts and will not place them at the disposal of the Church.

(iii) In papyrus Greek *proslambanesthai* has two specially significant usages. (*a*) It is used of 'welcoming a person into one's house and home'. When a person is received into the fellowship of the Church, he does not enter as a stranger into the midst of strangers; he enters as a member of a family into a family. Introductions are needless; there ought to be no strangeness to be bridged. The Church is a family, not a band of strangers who do not know each other. (*b*) In late Greek *proslambanesthai* is the technical term for 'enrolling a soldier into the army'. It is the word for receiving the enlisted man into the unit in which he is to serve. When a man enters the fellowship of the Church, he enlists in the army of Christ; he becomes a soldier of Christ.

This word *proslambanesthai*, the word of welcome and reception into the Christian Church, tells those who are inside the Church that they must welcome others as God welcomes them, that they must welcome them into the family of the Christian fellowship; and it tells those who enter that they must enter as allies and helpers, and as enlisted soldiers for the campaign of Christ.

PTŌCHOS

THE TRUE POVERTY

THIS word *ptōchos* is translated 'poor' in the AV of the Bible. That is a perfectly correct translation; but there is a wealth of meaning behind it. When Jesus read the lesson in the Synagogue at Nazareth, He chose the passage which said that the Spirit of the Lord was on the Servant of the Lord to preach the gospel to the 'poor' (Luke 4.18). When Jesus, as it were, stated His credentials to John's disciples, who had come asking if He really was the Anointed One,

His answering statement culminates in the words, The 'poor' have the gospel preached to them (Matt. 11.5). The Beatitudes begin with the saying: 'Blessed are the poor in spirit' (Matt. 5.3). In all these cases it is the word *ptōchos* which is used.

In Greek there are two words for 'poor'. There is the word *penēs*, which simply describes the man for whom life and living is a struggle, the man who is the reverse of the man who lives in affluence. There is this word *ptōchos*. This word comes from the verb *ptōssein*, which means to cower or crouch; and it describes not simply honest poverty, and the struggle of the labouring man to make ends meet; it describes abject poverty, which has literally nothing and which is in imminent danger of real starvation. First, then, let us note that *ptōchos* does not describe genteel poverty but real, acute destitution.

But behind this Greek word *ptōchos*, there lie two Hebrew words, the words *ebion* and *ani*. Both these words have a most interesting and significant development of meaning. Their meaning has three stages. (i) They mean simply 'poor', in the sense of lacking in this world's goods (Deut. 15.4; 15.11). (ii) They go on to mean, because poor, therefore 'downtrodden and oppressed' (Amos 2.6; 8.4). (iii) It is then that they take their great leap in meaning. If a man is poor and downtrodden and oppressed, he has no influence on earth, no power, no prestige. He cannot look to men for help and when all the help and resources of earth are closed to him, he can only look to God. And, therefore, these words come to describe people who, because they have nothing on earth, have come to put their complete and total trust in God (Amos 5.12; Ps. 10.2, 12, 17; 12.5; 14.6; 68.10).

We are now in a position to come at the real meaning of the Beatitude, 'Blessed are the poor in spirit'. (i) It means: blessed is man who has an utter sense of his own abject destitution in the sight of God, the man who feels not simply unsatisfactory, but who can only say, God be merciful to me, a sinner. (ii) But equally it means: blessed is the man who feels this sense of destitution and who has then put his utter and complete trust in God. So then the Beatitude means: blessed is the man who is conscious of a desperate need and who is utterly certain that in God, and in God alone, that need can be supplied. In the NT the 'poor' are those who realize their own abject helplessness and the wealth of the riches of the grace of God.

SKANDALON AND SKANDALIZEIN

THE STUMBLING-BLOCK IN THE WAY

Skandalon is the word which the AV regularly translates 'stumbling-block' or 'offence', and *skandalizein* is the corresponding verb. The interest of this word lies in the fact that it has, not one, but two pictures behind it, and to differentiate between the two will often give us a much more vivid picture.

The word *skandalon* is not a classical Greek word at all. It is late Greek and is, in fact, much commoner in the Septuagint and in the NT than anywhere else. The classical equivalent is *skandalēthron*, which means 'the bait-stick in a trap'. The *skandalēthron* was the arm or stick on which the bait was fixed. The animal for which the trap was set was lured by the bait to touch or step on the stick; the stick touched off a spring; and so the animal was enticed to its capture or destruction. In classical Greek the word is used by Aristophanes for 'verbal traps' set to lure a person in an argument into defeat. It is therefore clear that the original flavour of the word was not so much 'a stumbling-block' to trip someone up as an 'enticement' to lure someone to destruction.

When we turn to the Septuagint we find that this distinction is still quite clear. The Greek word *skandalon* is used to translate two Hebrew words. (*a*) It is used to translate the word *michsol*, which quite definitely does mean a 'stumbling-block'. It is so in Lev. 19.14, 'Thou shalt not put a stumbling-block before the blind.' It is so used in Ps. 119.165, 'Great peace have they which love Thy law:

and nothing shall offend them.' That is to say, 'Nothing shall trip them up.' (*b*) It is used to translate the word *mokesh*, which definitely means 'a trap' or 'a snare'. So in Josh. 23.13 alliances with foreign nations are said to be 'snares' and 'traps'. In Ps. 140.5 the Psalmist says that the proud have hid a 'snare' for him, and cords; they have spread a 'net' by the wayside; they have set 'gins' for him. In Ps. 141.9 the Psalmist prays: 'Keep me from the snares which they have laid for me, and the gins of the workers of iniquity.' In Ps. 69.22 the Psalmist says: 'Let their table become a snare before them; and that which should have been for their welfare, let it become a trap.' The idea is that success and prosperity can become a snare instead of a blessing. In the Septuagint, then, the word *skandalon* has two ideas behind it. It means either a 'stumbling-block', something set in a man's path to trip him up, or 'a snare', 'a bait', 'a lure' to entice him astray and so to ruin him.

When we turn to the NT we find that the translators of the AV always took *skandalon* in the sense of 'stumbling-block', but when we go to the NT passages with the idea of the double meaning of *skandalon* in our minds, we find that in certain passages the other meaning gives a more vivid picture.

(i) There are some passages where either meaning is perfectly suitable. In Matt. 13.41 it is said that the Son of Man will remove all *skandala* from His Kingdom. When the Kingdom comes all the things which are calculated to make a man sin, all the things which could trip him up, all the things which would entice him and seduce him into the wrong way will be taken away. The Kingdom will be a state of things in which temptation will lose its power.

(ii) There are some passages where the meaning of 'stumbling-block' is more fitting, or where it is even essential. In Rom. 14.13 we are forbidden to put a 'stumbling-block' or 'occasion to fall' in our brother's way. The word that is used for 'occasion to fall' is *proskomma*, which means 'a barrier', 'a hindrance', 'a road-block'. It is the word that would be used for a tree that has been felled and laid across a road to block it. We must never do or allow anything which would be a road-block on the way to goodness. In Matt. 13.21 the shallow hearer of the word is said to be 'offended' (*skandalizein*) by persecution. Persecution is a stumbling-block that stops him on the Christian way. The Pharisees are 'offended' by Jesus and His words (Matt. 15.12). Jesus forecasts that all His disciples will be 'offended' because of Him (Matt. 26.31). The false teachers put a 'stumbling-block' in the way of others (Rev. 2.14). The Jews find the cross of Christ 'a stumbling-block' and 'an offence' (I Cor. 1.23; Gal. 5.11). In all these cases, the words mean something which stops a man's progress, something which trips him up, something which bars the way to him. That something may come from the malicious action of others, or it may come from the prejudice and the pride of a man's own heart.

(iii) But there are certain cases where it gives a far better picture to take *skandalon* and *skandalizein* in the sense of a 'trap', a 'snare', a 'bait', an 'allurement', an 'enticement to sin'. Rom. 16.17 warns against those who cause devisions and 'offences' contrary to the doctrine which Christ's people have received. That is a warning against those who would 'lure' us from the way of true belief. I John 2.10 says: 'He that loveth his brother abideth in the light, and there is no *skandalon* in him.' That is to say, 'He would never entice and seduce anyone into sin.' Matt. 18.6 talks about the sin of 'offending' one of these little ones, and the next verse talks about the terribleness of 'offences'. It gives a much better picture to take *skandalon* and *skandalizein* there in the sense of luring and enticing the younger and the more impressionable people to sin. Matt. 5.29, 30 speak of the necessity of cutting off and plucking out the hand and the eye which 'offend' us. Clearly it is better there to take *skandalon* in the sense of 'that which lays a trap or snare to entice us into the ruin of sin'. If the desires of the hand and the eye are a bait to sin they must be eradicated.

When Burns went to learn flax-dressing in Irvine he met an older man who led him far astray. He said of him afterwards: 'His friendship did me a mischief.' That is precisely the meaning of *skandalon*. A *skandalon* is that which trips us up or that which lures us into sin. From our own lives such things must be rooted out; and God will not hold us guiltless if we bring such things into the lives of others.

SŌTĒRIA AND SŌZEIN

THE WORD OF SALVATION

In the Old Testament

THE noun *sōtēria* means 'salvation' and the verb *sōzein* means 'to save', and surely it is of paramount importance that we should find out what salvation and being saved mean. In classical Greek *sōtēria* means 'deliverance' or 'preservation'. It can be used for a man's safe return to his own home or his own country after an absence and a journey. It can mean a 'guarantee of safety' or a 'security against danger'. In the papyri by far the commonest meaning of *sōtēria* is 'bodily health'. For instance, a member of the family writes home, 'Write me a letter about your *sōtēria*,' or, as we would say, 'Let me know how you are.'

But it is only natural that we should look for the beginning of the meaning of *sōtēria* in the Septuagint, the Greek version of the OT scriptures, for it was on it that so many of the early Christians were nurtured. It was the Bible of the Church before ever the NT was written and it coloured the thoughts and the language of the early Church all the time.

(i) In the Septuagint *sōtēria* means at its simplest 'general safety and security'. In the multitude of counsellors there is *sōtēria*, says the proverb (Prov. 11.14). It is Jacob's bargain that if he comes again to his home in *sōtēria* Yahweh would be his God (Gen. 28.21). It is Joseph's promise that every man in whose sack the cup is not found shall return home in *sōtēria* (Gen. 44.17; cp. Gen. 26.31; Job 11.20; 13.16; 30.15).

(ii) In the Septuagint *sōtēria* means 'deliverance from trouble in general'. The mockers say to the Psalmist, 'There is no *sōtēria* for him in God' (Ps. 3.2). God is the *sōtēria* of the Psalmist's countenance (Ps. 42.11). He prays to God to command *sōtēria* (Ps. 44.4). The man who waits on God will rejoice in His *sōtēria* (Isa. 25.9; cp. Ps. 20.6; Isa. 38.20; Jer. 25.35).

(iii) In the Septuagint *sōtēria* specially means 'deliverance from an enemy'. In the AV it is represented by such words as 'salvation', 'help', 'escape', 'victory'. It describes deliverance from the Philistines (Judg. 15.18), from the Ammonites (I Sam. 11.9, 13), from Syria (II Kings 13.5), from Egypt (II Chron. 12.7), from Moab (II Chron. 20.17). It describes Israel's divine deliverance from her enemies through all her history.

(iv) In the Septuagint *sōtēria* specially describes 'Israel's deliverance at the Red Sea'. 'Stand still,' says Moses, 'and see the *sōtēria* of the Lord which he will show to you to-day' (Ex. 14.13). Every deliverance was a *sōtēria* of the Lord, but the deliverance at the Red Sea was the *sōtēria par excellence.* There above all God's hand was seen in all its splendour and its strength.

(v) Sometimes in the Septuagint this *sōtēria* is 'eschatological', that is to say, it will find its full flowering and glory only in the new age which is to come. It is not something which exhausts itself in this world. It will be mighty to save in any world that will ever be (Isa. 45.17; 52.10; Jer. 3.23).

(vi) Consistently this *sōtēria* is connected with and attributed to God. Contrasted with it 'vain is the help of man' (Ps. 60.11; 108.12; 146.3). It is God who is characteristically the God of *sōtēria,* the God of 'salvation' (Ps. 18.46; 38.22; 51.14; 88.1). When the power of man is helpless, the *sōtēria* of God steps in. Man's extremity is always God's opportunity.

(vii) Lastly, we may note that this word *sōtēria* has a way of appearing in the midst of triumphant lyrical passages of singing thanksgiving. It appears in the Song of Moses after the crossing of the Red Sea (Ex. 15.2), in the Song of David after his deliverance from Saul (II Sam. 22.3, 36, 47, 51), in the Song of Hannah when she knew she was to have a son (I Sam. 2.1). It makes the man who experiences it sing for very joy.

So, then, the NT writers when they used *sōtēria* entered into a rich heritage, for already it described the saving, preserving, providential power of God in the crises of history and the crises of the individual life, a care which does not stop with this world, and a care which makes the man who is wrapped round by it sing with joy.

In the New Testament

Two of the older uses are repeated in the NT.

(i) *Sōtēria* is used of 'deliverance from enemies' (Luke 1.69, 71; Acts 7.25; Jude 25). It is to be noted that all these passages have a characteristically OT background.

(ii) Both noun and verb are used of 'bodily health and safety' in the NT. They are used of Paul's preservation in shipwreck (Acts 27.20, 34) and of Noah's construction of the ark for the saving of himself and of his family (Heb. 11.7).

But, having noted these older usages, we must now come to the distinctive and characteristic NT usages of these words.

(i) *Sōtēria* is 'the aim of God' and 'the purpose of Jesus Christ'. The NT knows nothing of an angry God who has to be pacified into forgiving men. It knows nothing of a God whose attitude to men has somehow to be changed from wrath to mercy. In the NT the whole initiative of *sōtēria* is with God. God has not appointed us to wrath but to obtain *sōtēria* (I Thess. 5.9). God has from the beginning chosen men to 'salvation' (II Thess. 2.13). God will have all men to be 'saved' (I Tim. 2.4). It is the long-suffering of God which makes *sōtēria* possible (II Pet. 3.15). It is according to God's mercy that we are 'saved' (Tit. 3.5). So much so is *sōtēria* a prerogative of God that it is ascribed to Him in the doxologies of the Revelation (Rev. 7.10; 19.1). It is God Himself who has 'saved' us (II Tim. 1.9). Christ Jesus came into the world to 'save' sinners (I Tim. 1.15). He came not to condemn the world, but that through Him the world might be 'saved' (John 3.17). The prime mover in *sōtēria* is God.

(ii) For this very reason *sōtēria* may be refused. It is something which has to be worked out with fear and trembling (Phil. 2.12). Great as it is, it can still be neglected (Heb. 2.3).

The NT never forgets that the perilous free-will of man can frustrate the saving purpose of God.

(iii) The place of Jesus in God's *sōtēria* is central. In no one else is *sōtēria*, and there is no other name in heaven or earth by which men may be saved (Acts 4.12). He is the *archēgos*, the pioneer, the trail-blazer of *sōtēria* (Heb. 2.10). He is the *aitios*, the moving and essential cause of *sōtēria* (Heb. 5.9). Without Himself and His work *sōtēria* is not possible.

(iv) None the less He needs His human agents. It is Paul's aim to do something to 'save' some of the Jews (Rom. 11.14). He is all things to all men that he may 'save' some (I Cor. 9.22). He exhorts the believing partner in marriage not to leave the unbelieving one for perhaps the believer may 'save' the unbeliever (I Cor. 7.16). Paul's whole desire in God's sight is to 'save' men (I Cor. 10.33). He blames the Jews for hindering him in this work (I Thess. 2.16). Timothy is to take heed to himself and his teaching that he may 'save' himself and others (I Tim. 4.16). The man who converts a sinner 'saves' a soul from death (Jas. 5.20). Jesus Christ needs lips to speak for Him, hands to work for Him, men to be His heralds.

(v) For this very reason the Christian message is certain things.

(*a*) The Christian message is 'the word of salvation' (Acts 13.26; Eph. 1.13). It is the good news of God's good will to men.

(*b*) The Christian message is 'the way of salvation' (Acts 16.17). It shows a man the path that leads to life and not to death.

(*c*) The Christian message is 'the power of salvation' (Rom. 1.16). It brings a man not only a task but also the strength to do it, not only a way but also the power to walk it, not only an offer but also the power to grasp it.

(*d*) The 'aim' of the Christian message is salvation (Rom. 10.1; II Cor. 6.1). The aim of the Christian message is not to hold a man over the flames of hell but to lift him up to the life of heaven.

We must now look at what we might call the NT elements of *sōtēria*, the things which bring 'salvation'.

(i) *Sōtēria* involves 'repentance'. A godly sorrow produces a repentance that works towards salvation (II Cor. 7.10). *Sōtēria* is something which has to be worked out with 'fear and trembling' (Phil. 2.12).

(ii) *Sōtēria* involves 'faith' (Eph. 2.8; II Tim. 3.15; I Pet. 1.9). It involves taking God at His word and casting oneself in utter trust on the offered mercy of God. It involves 'belief' (Rom. 1.16), the conviction that the promises of God in Christ are true, the willingness to stake one's life on the veracity of Jesus Christ. It involves 'hope' (Rom. 8.24). The repentance, the fear and trembling are not meant to move a man to despair but to move him to seek in radiant hope the remedy in Jesus Christ. Faith, hope and belief are all closely interlinked. They are all different expressions of the trust on which *sōtēria* is founded.

(iii) *Sōtēria* involves 'endurance'. It is he who endures to the end who will find *sōtēria* (Matt. 10.22; 24.13). The man who is daunted neither by opposition from without nor discouragement from within will in the end find salvation. He must be defeated neither by his own doubts nor by the arguments and seductions of others. His trust is something to which he must cling as to a life-belt in an overwhelming sea.

(iv) *Sōtēria* involves 'the love of truth' (II Thess. 2.10). It is something that the man who does not love the truth can never find. If a man shuts his eyes to the truth about himself he cannot be moved to the essential repentance. If he shuts his eyes to the truth about Jesus Christ he can never realize the finality of God's offer. And it is always true that there are none so blind as those who will not see.

(v) *Sōtēria* sometimes involves 'fear' (Jude 23). There is such a thing as a cleansing fear (Ps. 19.9). The fear of the Lord is the beginning of knowledge (Prov. 1.7). There is what someone has called 'the celestial shudder', the sudden spasm of fear at what we are, which drives us to find the hope of what in Christ we may be.

(vi) *Sōtēria* always involves 'grace'. It is founded on grace. By grace we are saved (Eph. 2.5). It was the conviction of the early Church that it was by the grace of the

Lord Jesus Christ that they were saved (Acts. 15.11). The sorrow of repentance, thc shudder of fear, is met by the grace of the Lord Jesus Christ, and the very word is the final proof that *sōtēria* is a gift which we have not earned and could not earn but which comes to us from the sheer goodness and generosity of God.

(vii) *Sōtēria* involves 'the message of the cross' even if that message seems at first hearing foolishness (I Cor. 1.18), and it involves the fact that we must never forget that message, that it must remain printed for ever on our memories (I Cor. 15.2). It involves the sight of the cross and the constant memory of the cross, the realization of the love of God and a life lived in that realization.

(viii) The writer to the Hebrews alone has one further thing to say. He would say that *sōtēria* involves 'the continued work of Christ'. It is his vision that Christ ever liveth to make intercession for us (Heb. 7.25). With one of the greatest reaches of thought in the NT he still sees Christ pleading for men, carrying on His high priestly work, and still opening the way to God for men, the vision of a Christ who loved us from the first of time and who will love us to the last, and whose continued love is our eternal hope of *sōtēria*.

In many cases in the NT *sōtēria* occurs as it were without explanation and without qualification. It is used as a word of whose meaning everyone would understand at least something. Such passages are Luke 19.9; Acts 11.14; 16.30; I Cor. 3.15; II Cor. 2.15).

But if we are to get the full value and the full meaning out of this word, we must ask the question: What is a man saved from? What is the deliverance which *sōtēria* promises? Before we begin to examine the NT for this purpose we must note one thing. The verb *sōzein* means both to save a man in the eternal sense, and to heal a man in the physical sense. Salvation in the NT is 'total salvation'. It saves a man, body and soul.

(i) *Sōtēria* is salvation from 'physical illness' (Matt. 9.21; Luke 8.36, in both of which cases the verb is *sōzein*). Jesus was concerned with men's bodies as well as with men's souls. It is significant that the Church is rediscovering that to-day. Such salvation may not cure, but it always enables the sufferer to transmute the suffering into glory.

(ii) *Sōtēria* is salvation from danger. When the disciples were in peril they cried out to be 'saved' (Matt. 8.25; 14.30). This does not mean protection from all peril and from all harm, but it does mean that the man who knows that he is within the *sōtēria* of God knows, as Rupert Brooke had it, that he is 'safe when all safety's lost'. It is the conviction that nothing in life or in death can separate him from the love of God.

(iii) *Sōtēria* is salvation from 'life's infection'. A man is saved from a crooked and perverse generation (Acts 2.40). The man who knows the *sōtēria* of God has within him and upon him a prophylactic quality, a divine antiseptic which enables him to walk in the world and yet to keep his garments unspotted from the world.

(iv) *Sōtēria* is salvation from 'lostness'. It was to seek and to save the lost that Jesus came (Matt. 18.11; Luke 19.10). It was to rescue a man when he was on the way to a situation in which he would lose his life and lose his soul. It was to turn him from the way that led to the most deadly kind of death to the way that led to the most vital kind of life.

(v) *Sōtēria* is salvation from 'sin'. Jesus was called Jesus because He was to save His people from their sins (Matt. 1.21). By himself man is the slave of sin. He cannot liberate himself from it. He can diagnose his situation easily enough, but he cannot cure his disease. The saving power of Christ alone can do that. 'He breaks the power of cancelled sin. He sets sin's prisoner free.'

(vi) *Sōtēria* is salvation from 'wrath' (Rom. 5.9). The NT cannot be emptied of the conception of judgment. That conception is fundamental to it. Jesus Christ did something, God did something, which freed men from the wrath of injured holiness and transgressed justice. In Jesus Christ something happened which put a man into a new relationship with God.

(vii) One last thing we may note. *Sōtēria* is eschatological. That is to say, we can begin to enjoy it here and now, but its full impact and its full wonder will only come to us in the day when Jesus Christ is enthroned King of all the world (Rom. 13.11; I Cor. 5.5; II Tim. 4.18; Heb. 9.28; I Pet. 1.5; Rev. 12.10). It is quite true that the Second Coming of Christ is not a popular doctrine. But it does conserve the tremendous truth that this world is going somewhere, and when the world reaches its final consummation so will *sōtēria* be finally perfected.

Sōtēria is that which saves a man from all that would ruin his soul in this life and in the life to come.

XENOS, PAREPIDĒMOS AND PAROIKOS

THE CHRISTIAN AND THE WORLD

THERE is a group of NT words which have come to be epitomes of the Christian attitude to the world. They all describe a person who is a pilgrim, a sojourner, a stranger and not a permanent resident in a place.

The first of these words is the word *xenos*. In classical Greek *xenos* means a 'stranger' or a 'foreigner'; it is contrasted with *politēs,* a 'citizen' of the country, with *epichōrios,* an 'inhabitant' of the land, and with *endēmos,* a 'native' of the country. It can even mean a 'wanderer' and a 'refugee'.

In the NT it is used of the 'stranger' in the parable to whom help was or was not given (Matt. 25.35, 38, 43, 44). The field which was bought with the blood-money which Judas Iscariot flung back to the priests is to be a burying-ground for 'strangers' (Matt. 27.7). The Athenians were interested in Paul because he preached 'strange' gods (Acts 17.18). The citizens of Athens and the 'strangers' who lived there were fascinated by all things new (Acts 17.21). Before Paul's Gentile converts were converted they were 'strangers' to the covenants of promise (Eph. 2.12), but now they are not 'strangers' any more. Those to whom the Epistle to the Hebrews was written are to beware of 'strange' doctrines (Heb. 13.9). Peter tells his friends not to regard the things that are happening to them as some 'strange' experience (I Pet. 4.12). John contrasts the brethren and the 'strangers' (III John 5). But the passage which gives the word its tone and meaning in Christian thought is the passage in Hebrews where the patriarchs were said to be 'strangers' and pilgrims all their lives (Heb. 11.13). Even so, the Christian is a *xenos,* a stranger in this world.

In the ancient world the 'stranger' had an uncomfortable time. In the papyri a man writes that he was despised by everyone 'because I am a *xenos,* a stranger'. Another writes home to tell his people: 'Do not be anxious about me because I am away from home, for I am personally acquainted with these places and I am no *xenos,* stranger, here.' Another writes: 'It is better for you to be in your own homes, whatever they may be like, than to be *epi xenēs,* in a strange land.' In the ancient world clubs in which the members met to have a common meal were very common; and those who sat down were divided into *sundeipnoi,* fellow-members, and *xenoi,* outsiders, who are guests only on sufferance and by courtesy. A mercenary soldier who was serving in a foreign army was *xenos,* a stranger (Xenophon, *Anabasis,* 1.1.10). In Sparta the 'stranger' was automatically regarded as a 'barbarian'. *Xenos* and *barbaros* meant one and the same thing (Herodotus 9.11).

Here then we have the truth that in this world the Christian is always a stranger; in this world he is never at home; he can never regard this world as his permanent residence. And just because of that he will always be liable to be misunderstood; he will always be liable to be looked upon as a strange character, who follows queer ways which are not the ways of other people. So long as the world is the world, the Christian must remain a stranger in it, because his citizenship is in heaven (Phil. 3.20).

The second word which describes the Christian's position in the world is the word *parepidēmos.* In classical Greek *parepidēmos* was the word for a person who had settled temporarily in a place without making it a permanent place of residence. In the NT it is used of the patriarchs, who never had a settled residence, but who were strangers and 'pilgrims' (Heb. 11.13). Peter uses it to describe the Christians who lived in Asia Minor; they were 'strangers' scattered throughout the country; they were exiles from home (I Pet. 1.1). His appeal to his people is that they should abstain from fleshly lusts which attack the soul, because they are strangers and *pilgrims* (I Pet. 2.11).

This word is used in the same way in the Septuagint. When Sarah died Abraham went to the children of Heth to ask for land wherein to bury her. He said: 'I am a stranger and a *sojourner* with you: give me a possession of a burying-place with you, that I may bury my dead' (Gen. 23.4). The Psalmist speaks of himself as a stranger and a sojourner as all his fathers were (Ps. 39.12).

The Greeks who lived at Rome called themselves *parepidēmoi* (Polybius 32.22.4). In the papyri a man asks for permission *parepidēmein pros kairon*, to reside temporarily in a place for a certain time; and another man is given permission to stay but he must not *parepidēmein* for more than twenty days; his temporary residence must not exceed that length of time.

The Christian is essentially a temporary resident in this world. He is a person who is essentially on the way. He may be here but his roots are not here, and his permanent home is not here. He is always living as one who is looking beyond. It so happens that this view of life was not uncommon in the great Greeks. Marcus Aurelius (2.17) said: 'Life is a warfare and a sojourn (*parepidēmia*) in a foreign land.' Diogenes Laertius (*Lives of the Philosophers*, 2.3.7) tells of a saying of Anaxagoras: 'He was eminent for wealth and noble birth, and furthermore for magnanimity, in that he gave up his patrimony to his relations. For, when they accused him of neglecting it, he replied: "Why then do you not look after it?" And at last he went into retirement and engaged in scientific investigation without troubling himself about public affairs. When someone inquired: "Have you no concern in your native land?" gently, he said, "I am greatly concerned with my fatherland," and pointed to the sky.' Epictetus (2.23.36 ff.) draws a picture of life as he sees it: 'Men act like a traveller on the way to his own country, who stops at an excellent inn, and, since the inn pleases him, stays there. Man, you have forgotten your purpose; you were not travelling *to* this but *through* it. "But this is a fine inn." And how many other inns are fine, and how many meadows—yet simply for passing through.' Epictetus saw the world, not as the destination of the journey, but as an inn upon the way.

The word *parepidēmos* describes a man who is passing a temporary sojourn in a place, but who has no permanent residence there. The Christian does not despise the world, but he knows that for him the world is not a permanent residence but only a stage upon the way.

The third word which describes the relationship of the Christian to the world is the noun *paroikos,* with its verb *paroikein.* In classical Greek the word is more usually *metoikos,* and it describes what was known as a 'resident alien'. The resident alien was a man who came to stay in a place without being naturalized. He paid an alien tax; he was a licensed sojourner. He stayed in some place, but he had never given up citizenship of the place to which he truly belonged.

In the NT the word is used several times. God told Abraham that his descendants would 'sojourn' in a strange land (Acts 7.6). Moses was a 'stranger' in the land of Midian (Acts 7.29). On the road to Emmaus the two travellers ask the unrecognized risen Christ if He is only a 'stranger' in Jerusalem because He does not seem to know of the tragedy that has happened (Luke 24.18). When the Gentiles enter the Christian faith they are not 'strangers' to God's promises any more. But once again it is Hebrews and I Peter which give this word its special tone and emphasis and meaning. Once again Hebrews describes the patriarchs as 'sojourners', with no permanent residence (Heb. 11.9); and it is Peter's appeal that his people should keep themselves clean because they are strangers and 'pilgrims' (I Pet. 2.11).

The word *paroikos* occurs often in the Septuagint. Eleven times it translates the Hebrew word *gēr;* the *gēr* was the stranger, the proselyte, the foreigner who was a dweller within the family of Israel. Ten times it translates the word *tōshab*; the *tōshab* was the emigrant sojourning in a strange country, where he is not naturalized.

Thucydides uses the word *metoikos* to describe 'strangers' who have settled in Athens but who have never become citizens (2.13). Herodotus uses it of people in Crete who are settlers there, but not citizens of the country (4.151). It is the word which is regularly used in contrast with *politēs*, the full citizen of a country and with *katoikos*, the man who has his permanent residence there. A Carpathos inscription divides the population into two classes—*politai* and *paroikoi*, citizens and resident aliens. The governor of Priene invites to a festival *politai*, the 'citizens', *paroikoi*, the 'resident aliens', *katoikoi*, those who have their permanent residence in the town, and *xenoi*, the 'strangers' who happen to be there. The ancient world well knew the term *paroikos*; it described a man who lived within a community but whose citizenship was somewhere else.

The words were particularly used of the Jews of the Dispersion. The Jews were said *paroikein* in Egypt and in Babylon and in the lands outside Palestine to which they went by force or by choice. To the Jew the words described a person who lived within a community and who was yet a stranger within it.

It so happened that this word became specially connected with the Christian and with the Christian Church. The Christian was exactly in this position—he lived in a community, and he undertook all the duties of that community, but his citizenship was in heaven. Clement writes his letter from the Church *paroikousē* (the present participle) at Rome to the Church *paroikousē* at Corinth. Polycarp uses the same way of speaking when he writes to the Church at Philippi. The Church was in these places, but the true home of the Church was not there. Now there comes a very interesting development. The word *paroikos* means a 'resident alien'; the verb *paroikein* meant to stay in a place, but not to be a naturalized citizen of it. So the noun *paroikia* came to mean 'a body of aliens in the midst of any community'; and it is from this word *paroikia* that the English word 'parish' is derived. The Christian community is a body of people who live in this world, but who have never accepted the standards and the methods and the ways of this world. Their standards are the standards of God. They accept the law of the place wherein they dwell, but beyond them and above them, for them there stands the law of God. The Christian is essentially a person whose only real citizenship is citizenship of the Kingdom of God.

The idea of the Christian as a stranger and a pilgrim in the world became so much part of Christian thought that it is worth while to consider it a little further.

(i) In the ancient world to be a stranger in a strange place was to be unhappy. It is true that there was respect for the stranger. In Greek religion one of the titles of Zeus was *Zeus Xenios*, 'Zeus, the god of strangers'; and strangers were held to be under the protection of the gods; but none the less there was a certain wretchedness in the lot of the stranger. *The Letter of Aristeas* (249) has it: 'It is a fine thing to live and to die in one's own land; a foreign land brings contempt to the poor, and to the rich it brings suspicion that they have been exiled because of some evil they have done.' Ecclesiasticus (29.22-28) has a famous and wistful passage about the lot of the stranger:

Better the life of the poor under a shelter of logs,
  Than sumptuous fare in the house of strangers.
With little or with much, be contented;
  So wilt thou not have to bear the reproach of thy wandering.
An evil life it is to go from house to house,
  And where thou art a stranger thou must not open thy mouth.
A stranger thou art in that case, and drinkest contempt;
  And besides this thou wilt have to bear bitter things:
'Come hither, sojourner, furnish my table,
  And if thou hast aught feed me therewith';
Or, 'Get thee gone, sojourner, from the face of honour,
  My brother is come as my guest, I have need of my house'.
These things are grievous to a man of understanding:
  Upbraiding concerning sojourning, and the reproach of a money-lender.

The very fact that the Christian is a stranger and a pilgrim and a sojourner is the proof that comfort is the last thing that he can expect in life, and that an easy popularity is not for him.

(ii) This idea of the Christian as a stranger in the world is deeply rooted in the literature of the early Church. Tertullian wrote: 'The Christian knows that on earth he has a pilgrimage, but that he has his dignity in heaven' (*Apology*, 1). 'Nothing is of any importance to us in this world except to depart from it as quickly as possible' (*Apology*, 41). 'The Christian is a sojourner amongst corruptible things' (*The Letter to Diognetus*, 6.18). 'We have no fatherland on earth' (Clement of Alexandria, *Paedagogos*, 3.8.1). 'We are sojourners, unable to live happily exiled from our fatherland. We seek for a way to help us to end our sorrows and to return to our native country' (Augustine, *Concerning Christian Doctrine*, 2.4). 'We should consider, dearly beloved brethren, we should ever and anon reflect that we have renounced the world, and in the meantime are living here as guests and strangers. Let us greet the day which assigns each of us to our own home, which snatches us hence, and lifts us from the snares of the world, and restores us to Paradise and to the Kingdom. Who that has been placed in foreign lands would not hasten to return to his own country? Who that is hastening to return to his friends would not eagerly desire a prosperous gale, that he might the sooner embrace those dear to him. We regard Paradise as our country' (Cyprian, *Concerning Mortality*, 26).

(iii) At the same time it is to be noted that, although the Christians regarded themselves as strangers and pilgrims and exiles, that did not mean that they divorced themselves from ordinary life and living, and retired into a life of detached and isolated uselessness and inactivity. Tertullian writes: 'We are not like Indian Brahmins or gymnosophists, exiles from ordinary life. We live like you pagans, enjoy the same food, manner of living and dress, and have business relations everywhere' (*Apology*, 42). The greatest of all expressions of this line of thought is in *The Letter to Diognetus*. 'Christians are distinguished from the rest of men neither by country nor by language nor by customs. For nowhere do they dwell in cities of their own; they do not use any strange forms of speech or practise a singular mode of life. . . . While they dwell in both Greek and barbarian cities, each as his lot was cast, and follow the customs of the land in dress and food and other matters of living, they show forth the remarkable and admittedly strange order of their own citizenship. They live in fatherlands of their own, but as aliens. They share all things as citizens, and suffer all things as strangers. Every foreign land is their fatherland, and every fatherland a foreign land. . . . They are in the flesh, but they do not live after the flesh. They pass their days on earth, but they have their citizenship in heaven' (op. cit. 5.1-9; H. G. Meecham's translation). It was by living in the world, and not by withdrawing from the world, that the Christians showed their true citizenship.

(iv) The matter may well be summed up in one of the unwritten sayings of Jesus. Dr. Alexander Duff, the Scottish missionary, was travelling in India in 1849. He journeyed up the Ganges and in the town of Futehpur-Sikri, which is twenty-four miles west of Agra, he came upon a Mohammedan mosque which is one of the largest mosques in the world. The gateway was one hundred and twenty feet high and wide; and inside the gateway on the right he noticed an inscription in Arabic. It read like this: 'Jesus, on whom be peace, has said: "The world is merely a bridge: ye are to pass over it, and not to build your dwellings upon it."' We may well believe that that saying did come from the lips of Jesus. To the Christian the world can never be an end and a goal in itself; the Christian is ever a pilgrim who is on the way.